100 Ideas for Primary Teachers:

Mindfulness in the Classroom

Other titles in the 100 Ideas for Primary Teachers series

100 Ideas for Primary Teachers:

Mindfulness in the Classroom

Tammie Prince

B L O O M S B U R Y

LONDON · OXFORD · NEW YORK · NEW DELHI · SYDNEY

Bloomsbury Education
An imprint of Bloomsbury Publishing Plc

50 Bedford Square
London
WC1B 3DP
UK

1385 Broadway
New York
NY 10018
USA

www.bloomsbury.com

First published in Great Britain 2017

A catalogue record for this book is available from the British Library.

ISBN:
PB: 9781472944955
ePub: 9781472944931
ePDF: 9781472944924

2 4 6 8 10 9 7 5 3 1

Typeset by Newgen Knowledge Works Pvt. Ltd., Chennai, India
Printed and bound by CPI Group (UK) Ltd, Croydon, CR0 4YY

To find out more about our authors and books visit www.bloomsbury.com.
Here you will find extracts, author interviews, details of forthcoming events
and the option to sign up for our newsletters.

Contents

Acknowledgements

Special acknowledgement and thanks go to the staff and children of Green Lane Primary for their support and enthusiasm in the development and trialling of the initial research for developing mindfulness in the classroom.

Thanks also go to my Twitter followers worldwide who continued to trial the strategies in the classroom and give constructive feedback during the writing of the book, and to the publishing team at Bloomsbury for their support and guidance.

Above all, I would like to thank my husband, Chris, for his support, patience and belief in me and the writing of this book. You keep me focused.

Introduction

According to the UK government document *Mental Health and Behaviour in Schools*, 'One in ten children and young people aged 5 to 16 has a clinically diagnosed mental health disorder and around one in seven has less severe problems'. One of the key points made in the document is that in order to help children succeed, schools have a role to play in supporting them to be resilient and mentally healthy.

The development of mindfulness in the classroom arms our children with lifelong skills that support their current and future mental health and well-being. Mindfulness can be defined as the mental state achieved by focusing on the present moment while also accepting our feelings, thoughts and bodily sensations. Studies have shown that childhood mindfulness development has numerous positive benefits. Some of these include stress relief, mental focus, discovering life balance, deepening social skills, better sleep, greater self-esteem, emotion control, improved decision-making skills and development of mathematical skills.

However, with an ever-growing curriculum, planning for yet another aspect within a school day can feel like an overwhelming task. Adding the shrinking budgets available for resourcing new initiatives in school has led to the development of this book to provide teachers in the classroom with free and low-cost ideas that are quick and easy to use to support the development of mindfulness. There is no need to follow any particular order or to use all of the strategies. You can pick and choose those that catch your interest and give them a try. It is suggested that you try a strategy at least two times before you dismiss it. This is particularly true with many of the breathing and meditation ideas.

The foundation of the book is to integrate mindfulness as part of the school day, taking into account the needs of the class and aiming to develop positive mental health skills for **ALL** children in the class, including those with ADHD and autism spectrum disorders.

Essentially, we want mindful practice to be part and parcel of our children's lives and something that they can take beyond the classroom doors and into the real world.

Once children have been taught many of the various strategies, they can be used as part of the scheduled day with little additional input or teaching. The key is that the children will start to use what they have been taught independently as a way of dealing with their own anxiety, stress, anger, etc. A positive impact can be seen with as little as ten minutes of mindfulness-based activity each day. It is important that, when you teach the strategies, all the adults who work with the children also know the strategies so that they can be understood and encouraged.

There is a section specifically for mindfulness strategies for adults included in the book. It is important to note that the number one factor in the success of the development of mindfulness in the classroom is the development of your own mindfulness.

Not all strategies will work for all people. Therefore, trialling a variety of strategies that you feel comfortable with delivering and trying out is important when finding just the right ones that meet the needs of you and your class.

Inhale deeply, hold, exhale completely and begin.

How to use this book

This book includes quick, easy, practical ideas and guidance for you to dip in and out of, to help you plan and carry out mindfulness activities for the children in your class.

Each idea includes:

- a catchy title, easy to refer to and share with your colleagues
- a quote from a practitioner, parent or child describing their experience that has led to the idea
- a summary of the idea in bold, making it easy to flick through the book and identify an idea you want to use at a glance
- a step-by-step guide to implementing the idea.

Each idea also includes one or more of the following:

Teaching tip

Practical tips and advice for how and how not to run the activity or put the idea into practice.

Taking it further

Ideas and advice for how to extend the idea or develop it further.

Bonus idea ★

There are 27 bonus ideas in this book that are extra exciting, extra original and extra interesting.

#hashtags

To prompt further exploration and discussion of the ideas online.

Breathing

Part 1

Deep breathing

'I knew breathing was important. But I never realised how important it can be for our mental well-being.'

Deep breathing is the basis of most mindfulness exercises, and nature's automatic response to calm a person down. It allows you to focus and stay grounded in the present moment.

We take more than 20,000 breaths a day. Breathing is as natural as you can get.

There is really no right or wrong way to deep breathe. However, a formula to follow is to inhale for a shorter time than you exhale, with a slight pause in-between and a slight pause at the end of each breath. You are trying to do two things: trick your body into thinking it is relaxed (even if it is not) and provide an anchor point in the present.

Focus during the breathing should be on the sound, feel and rhythm of your breath, particularly on the exhale.

When teaching this technique to children, it is important that you talk them through the breathing. Here is a short script you can try:

- **Breathe in 1, 2, 3, 4, 5** (modelling a slow, deliberate inhaling of breath that fills the body).
- **Pause** (pause only for a count of one, which is about as long as it takes for you to say the word).
- **Breathe out 1, 2, 3, 4, 5, 6, 7, 8** (modelling a slow, deliberate exhaling of breath that pushes out all the air from the lungs).
- **Pause.**
- Repeat as desired.

This is also useful to use when a child is angry, anxious or upset and unable to explain what the problem is.

Bonus idea ★

Mindful minute meditation: At the beginning or end of a lesson, or at any moment you want the class to stop and refocus, all of the children can do this together. Have the children stop, close their eyes and do 15 deep, mindful breaths together. Encourage them to focus on the air flowing in and out of their bodies. This will take about one minute. When finished, proceed in a quiet, mindful manner.

#DeepBreathing

Fingertip touch and breathe

'My more active children enjoy using this breathing idea because it allows them to keep moving but still focus on their breath.'

Even though breathing is a natural reflex, for those children who are more active, sitting breathing quietly is not enough. This repetitive exercise allows the child to focus while breathing deeply.

We all have those children who find sitting quietly extremely difficult. This is particularly true when they are younger or at the beginning of developing their mindful practice. The 'fingertip touch and breathe' technique is a repetitive exercise that allows the child to focus on one thing while using deep breathing to calm the mind.

The idea is simple:

- Ask the child to use their dominant hand and touch their thumb to their index finger while they inhale a deep, mindful breath (Idea 1).
- As they exhale, they touch their thumb to the middle finger.
- Inhale again, while touching their thumb to their ring finger.
- Exhale again, while touching their thumb to their little finger.
- Move the thumb back to the ring finger and inhale.
- Keep moving up and down the hand, touching thumb to finger with each inhale or exhale, until they are calm or for the given amount of time.

Children can either close their eyes or watch their fingers. The key is getting them to breathe deeply to kick in the natural relaxation reflex.

Teaching tip

Encourage the child to allow their shoulders to drop as they exhale. This will support the relaxation of the muscles that tend to hold tension, even in young children, and quicken the natural reflexes.

Taking it further

Sighing is an automatic bodily response that humans use to relax. Many people sigh without realising it is happening. Society has deemed this rude. Instead of reacting to it negatively, bring attention to the sigh and praise the child for using the sigh to calm themselves down. It is a far more positive way of dealing with the situation and may encourage more mindful, deep breathing.

#FingertipBreathing

Playful breathing

'There is absolutely no doubt my short mindfulness session on these breathing strategies had a direct impact on the lessons for the rest of the week. Instead of children getting upset with new learning, they were stopping and using their chosen breathing techniques.'

Breathing is a 'pack and go' mindfulness strategy that can be used in a variety of situations. Playful breathing gives children options for deep breathing that keep them engaged while also turning up the parasympathetic nervous system, which turns off the stress hormone pump.

Teaching tip

At first, teach one different breathing technique a week. Use it at the beginning of lessons, end of lessons, during transition times or when the children are restless. Use your imagination, as the whens and wheres are endless!

Belly breathing
Have the children sit or lie comfortably while placing their hands on their bellies. They should take a deep breath for four counts, blowing up their bellies like big balloons, hold their breath for one count, and then slowly exhale for five counts through their mouths, making the balloons deflate.

Snake breathing
Like a snake looking around, children should sit up tall and take a deep breath in for four counts, filling their bodies with the breath. They should pause for one count and then breathe out through their noses for five counts. Children enjoy making a hissing noise like a snake.

Bunny breathing
Children should imagine themselves as bunnies — bright-eyed, bushy-tailed and alert to their surroundings. They should sit on their shins with their backs straight, shoulders wide and chests lifted. Keeping their chins down, they take three big sniffs through their noses, one after another. When they exhale, they should release the air in one long sigh through their noses.

Bear breathing

Children should sit tall with closed eyes, imagining themselves as hibernating bears, sleeping peacefully in a cave for winter. Through their noses, they should breathe in for five counts, hold for three counts and then exhale through their mouths for a count of five.

Elephant breathing

What child has not imagined being an elephant, showering itself with its long trunk? The children should choose something to shower themselves with: love, laughter, strength, etc. They should stand with their feet wide apart, link their hands together and dangle their arms in front of them like an elephant's trunk, before inhaling deeply through their noses as they raise their 'trunks' high above their heads, and then leaning back and exhaling through their mouths as they swing their 'trunks' down to their legs. They should make sure they imagine themselves being showered by their thought of choice.

Birthday candle breathing

Every child enjoys their birthday and the anticipation of blowing out candles on their cake! For this breathing technique, children should sit with their legs crossed and backs straight. They should inhale deeply through their noses, stretching their arms up and out as they imagine seeing the birthday cake with burning candles in front of them. As they exhale through their mouths, as if to blow out the candles, they bring their arms back together at the centre of their chest.

#PlayfulBreathing

Breathing wand

'The children enjoyed making and using these fun breathing wands. They wanted to make one for everyone in their family!'

The breathing wand makes deep breathing fun for younger children which is important. The key is getting them to take deep breaths and BLOW all the air out of the lungs to kick in the natural reflexes.

As part of a lesson or area of provision, have the children make these fun, colourful and useful breathing wands.

You will need:
- cardboard tube (toilet roll or paper towel tube)
- tape
- scissors
- markers, crayons, paint, stickers and other bright and shiny bits and pieces to decorate the tube
- thin streamers and/or thin ribbon that can be easily moved by a child's breath.

How to make:
- Cut about 1cm off the top of the tube. Put this aside as you will need it later.
- Cut a straight line up through the remainder of the tube.
- Tighten the tube into a thinner tube and tape it at the top and bottom.
- Decorate the tube.
- On the smaller ring that was cut off the tube earlier, tape the thin streamers and ribbon around the inside edge.
- Tape this ring to the end of the decorated tube so it looks like a bubble wand.

Voila! You have a breathing wand!

Finally, take a deep breath and blow through the ring, making the streamers wave and flap.

Light as a feather

'The challenge of keeping the feather in the air really focuses the deep breathing in a fun and calming exercise.'

This is a cooperative breathing exercise that encourages deep breathing, as well as developing team building skills, concentration and active engagement.

Breathing releases toxins and tension, relaxes the body and mind and relieves emotional problems. This idea gives children opportunities during the day to breathe deeply, allowing them the space to refocus on the learning happening in the class.

You will need:
- a timer
- one small feather per pair/group (small down feathers work best)
- a space that is free from lots of wind or air movement.

How to:
- Divide the class into pairs or groups of three.
- Explain that the object of this 'game' is to keep the feather in the air without touching it.
- Discuss what types of breath will keep the feather in the air.
- Set the timer. I suggest 30 seconds in the beginning, increasing it each time the children do the exercise.
- After they have done it a few times, have the children discuss how they are feeling.
  - How do their bodies feel?
  - What emotions are they feeling?
  - How does it feel when they take that DEEP breath?
  - How does it feel at the end of an exhale when they have released all the breath?
- Repeat as appropriate for your class.

Taking it further

Once the children have done this exercise a few times and understand how deeply they must breathe and exhale to keep the feather in the air, incorporate this type of breathing as a visualisation (Idea 7) during transition times. Have the children sit up tall, close their eyes and visualise the feather floating in the air. In their minds, they are to keep the feather afloat with deep, mindful breaths for one minute.

#LightAsAFeather

STOP

'It's a really great tool to refocus the children when transitioning between tasks within a lesson or between lessons.'

Developing mindfulness has a lot to do with the shifting of perspectives. STOP is a simple but effective strategy to refocus the attention of the children.

Humans have some deeply laid neuropathways that allow us to fall into the habit of reactions. We don't even realise we are reacting; we just do it.

This ten-second mindful break is great for times when the class is getting a bit flustered, upset, noisy or otherwise not very mindful. It gives a moment for everyone in the class to consider what is happening around them and to relax for a short while.

You will need to teach them the following acronym:

S – Stop what you are doing.
T – Take a deep breath. Breathe in for a count of five, hold for a count of one and exhale for a count of eight.
O – Observe what is happening around you at this moment.
P – Proceed with what you were doing.

In the beginning, you will need to practise frequently, repeating the entirety of the acronym to reinforce what should be happening. In time, this will not be needed and, as soon as you signal, the children will be able to guide themselves through the exercise.

#STOP

Guided meditation

Part 2

Visualisation meditation

'I can't believe I used to go into a full day's teaching without doing this first thing in the morning. It's transformed the class's mindset.'

Visualisation meditation gives children a target to achieve for the day. By focusing on what they want to happen by the end of the day, the meditation allows them to be mindful of what they can do to achieve that target.

Visualisation allows for the development of self-belief, self-confidence and mental practice. It allows children to work out the steps for success.

Teaching tip

In the beginning, you will need to talk the children through the meditation. Over time, encourage them to guide themselves through the meditation by reducing your verbal cues until they are able to do it without any prompting.

- Play soft meditation music in the background.
- Sit up tall in a comfortable position and take three deep belly breaths while allowing the shoulders to relax.
- Softly close your eyes as you consider what your target is for the day ahead. It could be a target you are working on in maths, writing or reading. It could be a behavioural target, like trying something new, making a new friend or not giving up on something you find hard.
- Once you have decided on your target for the day, imagine yourself working towards the target.
  - What will you see?
  - What will you hear?
  - What things will you say or do to reach that target?
- Complete the visualisation by imagining achieving the target.
  - How do you feel?
  - How are others reacting?
- Finally, end the meditation by taking three deep belly breaths, smile and open your eyes.

#VisualisationMeditation

Body scan

'I pretend I am a robot scanning my body to find all the bugs!'

Children must be able to recognise the tension in their bodies and identify where that tension is being held, so that they can identify the mindfulness strategy to use. However, just the act of a body scan meditation does have its own calming qualities.

A quick scan of their bodies will help bring children awareness of how they are feeling without judgement. Whatever they feel, they should acknowledge, accept and move on. They should be happy to be able to be present in this moment.

Teaching tip

I like to get the children to imagine a beam of light slowly moving over their bodies, scanning it for worries, aches, pains, upset, stress or anxiousness.

- Have the children either sit comfortably with their hands in their laps or lie down with their arms to their sides.
- Play soft, gentle music in the background.
- Have them take a deep breath: breathe in for five counts, hold for one count and exhale for eight counts.
- Direct them to become aware of their body in a gentle voice.
- Instruct them to slowly move their awareness, noticing the different sensations in all their body parts: head, face, neck, chest, arms, hands, fingers, torso, legs, feet and toes. Remind them not to judge the sensations; just accept that they are there.
- Have the children remain at rest for a few more deep breaths, being aware of their body breathing.
- Discuss with the children how the body scan felt. What did they notice? How could this help them when they are angry, upset or anxious?

#BodyScanMeditation

Squish and relax

'I like how this helps children to release tension, making them feel very relaxed and ready for learning.'

'Squish and relax' meditation is a progressive muscle relaxation method that teaches children how to relax their muscles through a two-step process: tensing (squish) and then relaxing particular muscle groups. The exercise helps children to lower their overall stress levels and relax.

Teaching tip

Want a script? Use an internet search engine and look for 'progressive muscle relaxation script for children', or search on YouTube for 'progressive muscle relaxation for children'.

When we become anxious or angry, we tend to tense our muscles. This idea works to capitalise on that natural reflex by practicing it in order to mindfully relax. Getting children to practice the entirety of the sequence supports them in developing a habit where they will repeat the 'Squish and relax' strategy independently.

- Have the children either sit comfortably with their hands in their laps or lie down with their arms at their sides.
- Play soft, gentle music in the background.
- Have them take a deep breath: breathe in for five counts, hold for one count and exhale for eight counts.
- Direct them to become aware of their body in a gentle voice.
- Instruct them to slowly move their awareness, noticing the different sensations across their body:
  - face and nose – scrunch up tightly
  - jaw – bite down hard
  - arms and hands – squeeze tightly like they are trying to pick up a heavy weight
  - arms and shoulders – squeeze tightly like they are holding a heavy load
  - stomach – tighten their tummy like they are trying to get their belly button to touch their spine
  - legs and feet – squeeze tightly like they are trying to hold a ball between their knees

- whole body – squish their entire body as tightly as they can and, on release, allow their body to go limp.
- Hold all poses for a count of five and then release completely.
- Have the children remain at rest for a few more deep breaths, being aware of their body breathing.
- Discuss with the children how their bodies felt during and after the meditation.
  - What did they notice?
  - How could this help them when they are angry, upset or anxious?

Some children will find it more difficult to concentrate on the process as you move across the body. For those children, have them focus on just the squeezing and relaxing of the hands and add a sensory element to the practice by using dough.

- Have them hold a piece of dough in each hand.
- Instruct them to look at the dough. Ask them to notice the urge to squeeze it.
- Is the dough hot, warm or cold?
- How would they describe the colour of the dough?
- Notice the smell of the dough.
- Push a finger into the dough. Can they see their finger print? What does it look like?
- Once they have had a moment to explore the sensations of the dough, gently instruct them to take a deep breath, exhale and close their eyes.
- Guide them to tightly squeeze their hands into fists and focus on the feel of the dough as it squishes in the palm and through the fingers.
- Repeat several times, while also encouraging them to continue their mindful breathing.

> **Bonus idea** ★
>
> Use the sensory element of the dough to do a mini-meditation. Have the children take a small ball of the dough and roll it between their hands. Encourage them to focus on the feel of the dough in their palms as they take deep, mindful belly breaths.

#SquishAndRelax

Sounds meditation

'This is an effective and soothing meditation that the children enjoy.'

The sounds meditation allows children to specifically focus on the sounds being heard, thus developing key mindfulness skills while also developing an important educational tool – listening.

Teaching tip

Don't have time to make your own recordings? Search on YouTube for the particular environment you want, followed by 'sounds' – for example, 'ocean sounds'.

Taking it further

Use this as a part of a starter activity to introduce a new topic to the children that engages the senses and imagination.

- In preparation for this idea, spend some time in various locations recording the sounds of different surroundings: the seaside, your back garden, the city centre, a forest, etc. Recordings should be between two and five minutes in length.
- Explain to the children that they will be doing a sounds meditation. They will need to listen to the sounds in the recording and think about:
  - What loud sounds do they hear?
  - What soft sounds do they hear?
  - Are the sounds natural or man-made?
  - How do the sounds make them feel?
  - Where do they think these sounds are coming from?
- Have the children sit comfortably or lie down, take a few deep belly breaths and close their eyes.
- Play the recording. Softly encourage the children to focus on the sounds and how those sounds make them feel.
- Once the recording is finished, have them describe what they could hear and how it made them feel. Where do they think the recording was made?
- Reveal the answer, by either showing a video/picture of the place or telling the children where the sounds were recorded. How perceptive were they? How can we focus on just the sounds around us to calm ourselves down when we are feeling anxious, scared, upset or overexcited?

#SoundsMeditation

Meditation marathon

'The power of observation is a deeply mindful task. The mutual support and modelling supported the development of their practice.'

The Dalai Lama once said, 'If every eight year old in the world is taught meditation, we will eliminate violence from the world within one generation.' Though this quote is not backed by any scientific proof, it does make you think about the power of mindfulness. This idea combines meditation with the act of observation, which in itself is a mindful activity.

- Pair up the children. The pairs should be comfortable with each other but not to the point of distraction.
- Explain to the children that they will be doing a meditation marathon. 'Marathon' in this instance means long-lasting.
- Each pair will take turns doing deep breathing (see Idea 1), while the other observes their partner, watching how their body moves, how quickly they breathe and how their face looks.
- Each child will get 30 seconds of deep, meditative breathing. After 30 seconds, they will swap roles and the other child gets 30 seconds of deep, meditative breathing.
- Repeat as many times as you feel is appropriate for your class.
- Once finished, discuss how the deep breathing made them feel, both in body and in mind. Then discuss what it was like to observe the meditation. What did they notice about the other person when they were meditating? Did their body relax? What about their face? Did their breathing slow down? How did it make them feel to watch someone else meditate? Did it help them meditate better by observing someone else doing it as well?

Teaching tip

For some children, doing this as a whole class may be too much, and small-group or pair-only approaches may be more beneficial in the beginning.

Taking it further

Once children have become comfortable with this practice, combine it with Idea 12: My meditation to encourage the development of emotional intelligence.

#MeditationMarathon

My meditation

'This gave a purpose to writing while also having children consider a deeper understanding of their mindfulness meditations.'

Once children have been successfully meditating for a while, it is time for them to take the next step — creating their own meditations.

- Have the children identify their favourite types of verbal guided meditations. Are they visualisations, fantasy stories, positive mantras or some other type?
- Share a variety of guided meditation scripts with the class, encouraging them to look and identify aspects that are successful. What does a guided meditation author need to consider?
- Share the structure of a good guided meditation:
  - begin with comfort and deep relaxation — breathing and bringing focus
  - positive suggestion — consider what the person will get out of their meditation
  - main body — this is the part that guides the person through the meditation with well-described images or storytelling
  - conclusion — bring the meditation to a calm and peaceful end with a positive suggestion.
- Give the children time to plan and discuss their meditations with others before writing.
- Encourage speaking and listening skills by asking the children to practise in pairs, reading the meditation with their partner and giving pointers for improvement.
- Finally, give each child time to record their meditation in a quiet place.

#MyMeditation

Active meditation

Part 3

Starfish hand meditation

'I love seeing the children use this to relax. It's brilliant for younger children and fantastic for kinaesthetic learners.'

I have learned that, to support the development of mindful skills in children, we must try lots of strategies so that they can find the ones that work best for them. One simple strategy that works for lots of children (and adults) is the starfish hand meditation. It is a great way to divert and refocus the mind.

Teaching tip

Always remind and encourage children to use this strategy to focus and calm down, especially when you see them getting upset, angry, worried or anxious. Model it as required.

Bonus idea ★

The point between the thumb and index finger is considered to be an acupuncture point, called Union Valley. Stimulating this point by squeezing and massaging is supposed to help reduce muscle tension and relieve stress.

Model this strategy to children and get them to practise it while they are in a calm and relaxed state. Use it as part of your daily meditation first thing in the morning, with gentle music playing in the background. The key is for children to use it without prompting when they are anxious or upset.

- Close your eyes and breathe deeply.
- Spread your fingers on one hand out like a starfish.
- Take the index finger from your other hand and trace around your fingers and hand. Inhale deeply as you move up a finger and exhale completely as you move down the finger. Concentrate only on how it feels and let other thoughts float away.
- Switch hands and repeat the process, encouraging deep breaths and full exhalations.
- Continue until you feel relaxed and calm.

#StarfishHandMeditation

Pebble meditation

'This is an interesting meditation that I found really helped children deal with their emotions.'

Hands-on and creative mindful activities that involve both tangible objects and nature can be playful and fun while encouraging mindfulness. Thich Nhat Hanh developed a variation of this meditation for children to engage them in mindfulness.

Each child should collect four pebbles, rocks or shells before the meditation. (This could be part of Idea 88: Basic mindful walking.) Ensure that each child has something to store their pebbles in so that the meditation can be redone as often as desired.

Children sit up straight and relax. They should place the four pebbles in front of them. Children pick up each pebble one at a time and say:

- 'Breathing in, I see myself as a flower. Breathing out, I feel fresh.' Flower, fresh (three breaths) – the words 'flower, fresh' are repeated together quietly for three in and out breaths. Repeat with the three other pebbles.
- 'Breathing in, I see myself as a mountain. Breathing out, I feel solid.' Mountain, solid (three breaths).
- 'Breathing in, I see myself as still, clear water. Breathing out, I reflect things as they really are.' Clear water, reflecting (three breaths).
- 'Breathing in, I see myself as space. Breathing out, I feel free.' Space, free (three breaths).

Teaching tip

You can start and end the meditation with the ringing of a bell or chime. As the children learn the meditation, they can lead the class or others in the meditation.

Taking it further

After they become more confident in this meditation, encourage the children to come up with their own meditation for the four pebbles – for example, loving kindness, gratitude, friends, etc.

#PebbleMeditation

19

Mind jar meditation

'These have been a brilliant classroom addition. They work amazingly for helping children manage moments of anger.'

We all have emotions, and they can range from blissfully happy to desperate despair to full-blown anger. These and the other emotions that come between are mystifying and hard to control for children. The mind jar gives children a visual focus point to take control of their emotions.

How to make a mind jar:
- Find a clean jar or a small, clear drinks bottle.
- Fill the jar/bottle three-quarters full with warm water (not hot!).
- Add a few drops of food colouring of your choice.
- Add the glitter. (I like using the finest loose glitter I can find combined with glitter glue. The warm water helps to dilute the glue but the glue also thickens the water, allowing the glitter to stay suspended for longer.)
- Add water to fill the jar/bottle and close it tightly.
- Give it a good shake and watch the glitter swirl around the bottle and slowly settle.

Note: it can take several vigorous shakes to help the glitter mix and begin settling to the bottom.

How to use a mind jar:
- When the child is feeling upset, they should shake the jar and then set it down.
- As they watch the glitter swirling, encourage them to do deep belly breaths, allowing themselves to calm and settle as the glitter calms and settles.
- Repeat as needed.

#MindJarMeditation

Finger labyrinth meditation

'An excellent idea, with so many different opportunities for incorporation in the classroom.'

A finger labyrinth is similar to a full-sized labyrinth that you would walk, except on a much smaller and more portable scale. The user traces the path to the centre, using a finger rather than feet.

A labyrinth is not a maze; a maze has dead ends that are used to confuse and trick the mind. A labyrinth is a spiral course with a single, winding, unobstructed path from the outside to the centre that is used to calm and relax, and they have been around for over 4,000 years.

- Print a finger labyrinth for each child.
- Children should sit comfortably with the labyrinth in front of them and take deep breaths, relaxing and focusing on the entrance to the labyrinth.
- They should place the pointer finger from their non-dominant hand on the entrance. If they find this too awkward at first, have them use their dominant hand but, over time, they should keep trying their non-dominant hand. This helps keep the mind focused on the meditation, due to the challenge it presents.
- They should slowly trace the pattern of the labyrinth with their finger, allowing their mind to clear from extra thoughts and focus solely on following the path.
- They should stop momentarily at the centre of the labyrinth, taking deep breaths and observing how they are feeling.
- Then they should retrace their path out of the labyrinth.
- Finally, they should sit back, breathe deeply and relax, observing how they are feeling again.

Bonus idea 1

Walking labyrinth: Why not try making a large-scale outdoor labyrinth, using materials like skipping ropes or beanbags? Children can use a printed finger labyrinth as a guide or create their own from their imagination. Then they take turns walking the labyrinth with slow, deliberate steps.

Bonus idea 2

3-D finger labyrinth: A 3-D labyrinth can be made by gluing string on the lines of a printed finger labyrinth and covering it with layers of tissue paper and diluted PVA glue (three parts glue, one part water). Once it has dried, the grooves will be easily seen and felt.

#FingerLabyrinth

Meditation chain

'This was perfect for children who fidget and are unable to stay still.'

Sometimes meditation for children can be difficult when they have no concept of how long they have to meditate. The beads on a meditation chain can help a child keep track of how long they have been meditating and how much longer they will be meditating. It allows meditation to become tangible and focuses the child in the moment.

How to make a meditation chain:
- Each child will need 15 beads of the same size, one larger bead and a sturdy piece of string.
- Have the children string their beads – not too tight, as the bea·'s need a little space to slide – with the two ends attached like a bracelet or necklace.

How to use a meditation chain:
Children sit comfortably, take the larger bead in their hand as well as two mindful breaths to relax. Then, holding the meditation chain, take the first smaller bead, slide it over and do one of the following:
- **Breathing meditation:** Take a deep, mindful breath. Repeat with each bead until they reach the larger bead, and then take two deep, mindful breaths.
- **Positive affirmation meditation:** Choose a positive mantra to be repeated 15 times until they reach the larger bead, and then take two deep, mindful breaths. Examples: 'I am a kind person', 'I am loved by many people', 'I can do this'.
- **Positive memories:** Think of a positive memory. Repeat with a new positive memory for each of the beads until they reach the larger bead, and then take two deep, mindful breaths.

#ChainMeditation

Mindful eating

'Mindful eating is one way that allows a child to become aware of the positive and nurturing foods they eat by using their senses.'

The key to mindfulness is focusing on the present moment calmly and accepting the feelings, thoughts and bodily sensations, even when we are eating.

Give each child a raisin, slice of apple or orange, pomegranate seed, dried fruit or any food you wish. (Be sure your children have no allergies and the food isn't a choking hazard.)

Verbally guide the children through the exercise.

- **Have the children look at the food they will be eating.**
  - What do you notice?
  - What colour is it?
  - Is it small or large?
- **Have the children smell the food.**
  - What does it smell like?
- **Direct their attention to how it feels.**
  - Can you squeeze it?
  - Is it smooth, sticky or rough?
  - Is it warm or cold?
  - Does it make any sounds?
- **Have the children, very slowly, put the piece of food in their mouths but *not* chew it! Leave it on the tongue.**
  - How does it feel on the tongue?
  - Can you taste anything?
  - Does it smell differently in your mouth?
- **Have the children begin to chew slowly, one mindful chew at a time.**
  - Does the taste change?
  - How does it feel in the mouth?
- **Try to get them to notice when they swallow, and see how far they can feel the food going into their bodies.**
- **Discuss what they felt during the activity.**

Teaching tip

Try this with a number of different foods, either in one sitting or over a period of time.

Taking it further

Turn on some meditation music and allow children to write about their experience.

#MindfulEating

Mindful drinking

'This was a great meditation, which supports mindfulness development while also encouraging even the most reluctant child to drink water and really enjoy the process.'

Teaching children to enjoy the simple things in life is important and allows you to bring attention to the things we sometimes do on autopilot, focusing on the moment. The drinking meditation allows us to hydrate our bodies and focus better on the work at hand.

Teaching tip

Use this meditation as part of the transition times after break or a PE session.

Taking it further

If there is a time when the children have a special drink, like milk, juice or hot chocolate, guide them through the same meditation as a way for them to appreciate the differences in the taste of liquids.

#MindfulDrinkingWater

I know that some children do not like drinking water. However, children need to drink plain water for this meditation. It can be from the tap or from a bottle, but it does need to be unflavoured.

- Each child is to have a glass, cup or bottle of plain water.
- Have the children sit down comfortably with their water.
- They should take a sip while you guide them through the experience.
- Tell the children to allow the sip to linger in their mouths.
- Notice the temperature of the liquid against their tongue, cheeks, gums and palate. What can they taste? Is there a sweetness, bitterness, acidic or even slightly salty taste?
- Ask them to notice the sensations of the water being swallowed and flowing down their throats and into their stomachs.
- Repeat and continue to remind the children to be mindful of each sip, allowing themselves to be in the present moment of drinking their water.

Mindful listening

'A class favourite! They keep asking me if they will be doing mindful listening today.'

Children and adults alike can find the purposeful focus on being in the present moment extremely difficult. Our brains are humming with a million different thoughts. The adrenaline coming from this constant state makes us become addicted to what is causing us to feel this way. Basic mindful listening is simple and needs a minimum amount of equipment and time.

With this activity, you will need a special bell that you will use just for mindful listening. There are several meditation bell apps for free and there are also paid apps available, although musical triangles are just as effective. However, if you want to be more authentic, you can get an actual meditation bell.

- The children should sit comfortably and close their eyes.
- Ask them to take a few cleansing belly breaths to help relax.
- Explain to them that they are to listen to the bell and, when they stop hearing the sound, they should give you a signal – raising their hands, putting their heads down, etc.
- To round it off, talk the children through a couple of belly breaths and then begin the lesson.

You will find that children will intently listen to the bell, focusing only on the sound. At first, they may stop hearing the bell quickly. Over time, they will focus so hard on the sound that they will continue to hear it well after the sound has actually ended.

Taking it further

Once your children have firmly grasped this mindful listening activity, you can start including mindful listening in topic work. Make relevant recordings that fit into your class's learning: ocean waves, city noises, kitchen noises, etc. Have children listen mindfully to the recordings. Then, discuss the sounds heard and identify the place where this may have been recorded.

#MindfulListening

Wave bottle

'The movement of the water and oil is extremely soothing, and children are fascinated by the motion and will actively find our wave bottles to use when they feel the need.'

Watching the waves as they crash on a beach has a soothing, rhythmic quality that gives a visual focus to the present moment. Unfortunately, most schools are not located on a beach. However, the qualities of the soothing rhythm can be created in a wave bottle.

Teaching tip

The bottle can be shaken vigorously. This will create lots of oil bubbles swirling around. It will look similar to Idea 15: Mind jar and can be used in a similar fashion, allowing the bubbles to burst and settle. The oil and water WILL separate if left alone.

#WaveBottle

How to make a wave bottle:
- Find a clean, clear drinks bottle.
- Fill the bottle half-full with water. (Note: be sure to add the water first.)
- Add a few drops of blue food colouring, cover and shake.
- Add clear baby oil to fill the bottle to the top, put glue along the inside tread of the bottle cap and close tightly.

How to use a wave bottle:
- When the child is feeling upset, they should gently lean the bottle on its side and move it from side to side, making gentle waves.
- As they watch the waves, encourage them to do deep belly breaths, allowing themselves to calm and settle as the waves move.
- Continue until calm.

Mandala meditation

'The children loved this meditation and described the positive effects it had on their mood and emotions.'

The word 'mandala' is taken from the classical Indian language of Sanskrit and means 'circle'. The circle is the basis of a design that has intricate geometric shapes that draw attention to the centre, and that inspires quiet contemplation.

- Find a mandala that you find pleasing. Either make a copy for each child or have the mandala shown on the whole-class screen.
- Play a selection of meditation music for the length of time you want the children to meditate. Usually this is one minute per year of age, so a six-year-old will meditate for six minutes.
- Children are to sit comfortably and take three deep belly breaths.
- They should look at the mandala, focusing on the centre of the design while still breathing at a steady rate.
- Gently guide the children in a soft voice, letting them know it is okay for their gaze to wander to other parts of the mandala, noticing the designs, colours and ways the lines meet each other. As the meditation comes towards the end, encourage children to focus back on the centre.
- In the last 30 seconds of the meditation, have the children close their eyes and recreate the design in their minds, continuing even, steady breaths.
- Complete the meditation with three deep, mindful belly breaths.

Teaching tip

Use simpler-designed mandalas for a shorter meditation in the beginning and slowly work up to more minutes of meditation.

Taking it further

Children can colour their own drawn or pre-printed mandalas (Idea 60) or they can create their own mandalas as part of a nature walk and collection of items from nature.

#MandalaMeditation

Mindful handwriting

'The handwriting has greatly improved and the handwriting sessions are exceptionally calming!'

The rhythmic motion and repetition required for handwriting, particularly for joined-up/cursive writing, can lead to true focus on the present moment. This mindfulness strategy can easily be integrated into the handwriting expectations of your class with no additional time required during the normal day.

Teaching tip

You will still need to teach the children the appropriate letter formations. Mindful handwriting is for the times when they are practising independently.

The key to mindfulness in the classroom is that it really does become part and parcel of the class itself. It is not an add-on that takes extra time, but part of everyday life and mindful learning. The practice of handwriting can be a very mindful activity, as long as we take appropriate consideration of the task at hand.

- Play a selection of meditation music.
- Before picking up the pen/pencil, have the children sit up tall (as if they are puppets with string at the top of their heads, pulling them up straight) with their hands in their laps or on the table. They should take three deep belly breaths, focusing only on their breathing.
- Then they should begin writing. Gently remind them to focus on the movement of the pen/pencil and the marks they are making. Encourage them to recognise the feel of the movement and the vibrations created as the pen/pencil causes friction with the paper. Encourage the same rhythmic breathing as the writing flows.
- When the music ends, have the children put down their pen/pencil, put their hands in their laps or on the table and take three deep belly breaths.

#MindfulHandwriting

Cloud meditation

'On nice days, I find children lying on the ground during break times, quietly watching the clouds. Those are the calmest playtimes!'

Children have a natural mindfulness, particularly when it comes to nature. Their inquisitive minds allow them to focus on the details of nature, noting the lines, colours and movement of the outdoors. The cloud meditation capitalises on this natural inquisitiveness.

- Children should find a comfortable position outside. It can be sitting or lying down, as long as their viewpoint is of the clouds and they are comfortable.
- Begin by having them take five deep mindful breaths (the snake breaths are perfect for this – see Idea 3).
- Ask them to stare at the clouds. Guide them in the beginning with simple questions:
  - Are the clouds fluffy or thin?
  - Are they moving?
  - Are they taking shapes of things you know?
  - Are they all the same colour?
  - What about the blue sky behind them?
- Encourage this quiet thinking time for as long as you can, allowing for peaceful solitude as they observe and breathe.
- Once they are finished, discuss how they feel or how they felt. What were they thinking?
- Discuss how they can do this on their own to help them deal with their emotions and anxieties. Encourage them to use the strategy independently.

Teaching tip

Take some time to do a cloud meditation yourself, placing a camera in position to video the clouds as you meditate. Then you can use it in class if it is a rainy day.

#CloudMeditation

Mindful singing

'Singing lessons have never been so calm and enjoyable. Focusing on the mindfulness of the singing has added a new dimension to our lessons.'

Singing is made up of deep breaths and long exhales, which is a natural calming strategy. We also know that music can have meditative properties. Thus, we can develop a mindful technique that can calm and relax children while also bringing joy.

Taking it further

Add mindfulness-themed songs to the class song list. Take some time to discuss the meaning of the songs and how they can remind us to be mindful in our everyday lives.

Mindfulness is about being in the moment – allowing yourself to accept this moment without judgement or wallowing in the present. When teaching children the important life skill of mindfulness, we should endeavour to show children that mindful moments are all around them and that, with a little consideration, these moments can help them to relax and enjoy life more fully.

The act of singing brings joy to many and, with it being part of the curriculum, is another way to bring mindfulness to the forefront in an integrated way.

- Begin by having children sit up comfortably with their hands in their laps. Then have them take three deep belly breaths, bringing their attention to their breath.
- Explain to children that, while they are singing, they should take nice, deep breaths and focus on how the sound vibrates through their bodies.
- How does the sound feel in your mouth? Against your tongue? In your throat? In your chest?
- How does singing make you feel emotionally?

The key is to bring awareness to the moment of singing and bask in the joy of the sound without judgement.

#MindfulSinging

Time to refocus

'The random mindfulness strategies never fail to bring lots of excitement and anticipation, followed by a general calmness across the class.'

'Time to refocus' is a great way to return awareness to what is happening in the daily life of the class.

Prepare:
- On ten strips of paper, write out the refocusing activities found below or create your own, fold them up and put them in a jar.
- Set a timer to chime at ten intervals during the day.

Begin:
- When the timer chimes, have a child randomly select a refocusing task from the jar for the class to complete.
- Begin and end each task with a deep belly breath.
- When the task is completed, continue with the lesson.

Refocusing tasks (the focus for each task should last one minute):
- **Choose a sense:** Identify one sense and focus on that sense.
- **Listen:** Count how many different sounds you hear.
- **Strike a pose**: Choose one yoga pose and pretend to be a statue.
- **Colour:** Choose one colour to notice.
- **Breathe:** Choose one of your favourite breathing techniques and focus on the breath.
- **Sit up straight:** Straighten your back, pick up your head and relax your shoulders.
- **Count backwards:** Start at 60 and count backwards in unison.
- **Squish and relax:** Squish the muscles in your hands and arms and relax. Repeat.

Taking it further

At the end of the day, take time to discuss the refocusing activities that the children tried during the day. Discuss which ones they found the most useful and return them to the jar. Divide the children into small groups and have each group come up with a mindfulness refocusing task to try. Add it to the jar. Repeat the next day.

#TimeToRefocus

Mindful laughter

'I never realised how calming laughter could be.'

Laughter pulls on our deepest and strongest desires to be happy. This quirky strategy allows the inner child to come out, even in children.

Teaching tip

Set up appropriate base rules for your class before you begin. This may include not touching one another, keeping personal space and/or at least pretending to laugh in the beginning. Also, agree on the cue that demonstrates the laughter needs to come to an end.

Bonus idea ★

Smiling meditation: Play meditation music softly in the background as children get into their meditation poses. They should take three deep breaths as they close their eyes and visualise someone they love sitting opposite them smiling. They should continue to breathe deeply, allowing themselves to smile back at their loved one. Continue for two to three minutes, encouraging children to feel the warm energy coming from the smiles around them.

Laughter produces natural endorphins that improve mood, lower stress levels and support emotional well-being. Even fake laughter is known to increase the endorphins and, if you allow yourself, that fake laughter soon turns into real laughter.

The idea is to start laughing by pretending that something IS funny. No words are spoken but lots of gestures and deep belly laughing are essential. Children usually find this very easy. Their natural urge to laugh is strong.

End the session by having children sit with their hands in their laps, doing calm breathing with soft meditation music playing in the background.

Discuss with children how they felt before the session and how they feel now. Have them mindfully consider their emotions before, during and after the session, identifying the sensations they feel and the lasting effects of the session.

#MindfulLaughter

Gratitude

Part 4

Random acts of kindness

'Fun and uplifting for children and staff!'

Random acts of kindness (RAK) are a way for us to deliberately brighten another person's day by doing something thoughtful, nice and caring.

We are a world of moaners; whining and moaning about everything, from the weather to the government, is a favourite pastime of young and old alike. We focus on the bad and are surprised by the good. This leads to a vicious cycle of negativity, which then becomes the focus of our attention, and anything positive is seen as just a fluke or fleeting moment. By taking the time to be grateful and lingering in that moment, we start to be mindful of the good things in the world. We start to see more positive things; positivity breeds positivity. We start to see the good in people, we crave it and, when we see it, we want to repeat even more good.

- Discuss with children what a random act of kindness is and come up with a list of RAKs equal to at least the number of children in the class.
- Write these RAKs on individual slips of paper, fold them, put them into a hat/bag/bowl and allow each child to take one RAK. (NO TELLING! It is a secret!)
- Alternatively, each child can come up with their own RAK (they are more likely to be able to do this after they have had more practice of RAKs).
- During the given time frame, each child is to complete the act WITHOUT saying that they are completing the RAK. (This will also take some time as, at first, they will want to tell everyone what they have done. The point of RAKs is to do a RAK without recognition.

That will be the ultimate level of this mindful practice.)

- After the given time frame, discuss as a class how completing the RAK made them feel and how they think it made the other person feel.

Here are some ideas for RAKs to get you started, some aimed at children and some for adults:

- Make a 'thank you' card for someone, thanking them for their love, caring, help or any other thing that person has done for you.
- Do a chore for a sibling or parent without being asked.
- Smile at a stranger who is looking sad.
- Tweet or Facebook message a genuine compliment to three people.
- While you're out, compliment a parent on how well-behaved their child is.
- When everyone around you is gossiping about someone, be the one to say something nice.
- Write a positive note and leave it in a random place to be discovered.
- Email or write to a person who has made a difference in your life.
- Let someone into your lane on your way to or from work.
- Give someone an unexpected hug!

Bonus idea ★

Make RAK a family or school challenge! Set a time frame, promote the initiative to build up excitement and then declare it #RandomActs OfKindness day or week! Get children, staff, families and communities to put it on social media, write about it in class and spread the positivity!

#RandomActsOfKindness

Say 'cheese'!

'Children began noticing good qualities in others and, after this exercise, I noticed that they were giving each other compliments more often.'

'Say "cheese"' is a mindful appreciation activity. Appreciation is the recognition and enjoyment of the good qualities of someone or something.

Taking it further

Showcase the messages on a display board or put them together to form a class book. Encourage the children to refer to them when they are feeling down about themselves and to write additional messages for others during the year.

Mindfulness allows us to have the ability to have a deep sense of appreciation. This allows us to have mindful gratitude which can bring us peace, as well as increase our awareness of what we have around us.

- Take a picture of each child and create a sheet with their picture in the middle. Leave enough room around the picture so that several children can write messages around the edge.
- Discuss with the children what the word 'appreciation' means and that appreciation can be shown for others as well as ourselves (inner appreciation). (This can sometimes be hard for children. Encourage lots of talk about inner appreciation in the discussion.)
- Give each child the sheet with their picture on it. They should write one thing they appreciate about themselves and sign their name.
- Deciding on a plan of rotation that best fits your class, have the children take a child's sheet and write a message of appreciation to the pictured child and sign their name.
- When finished, ensure that each child gets their sheet back and has time to read the messages. Encourage children to share their own favourite message with the class and describe how it makes them feel.

#SayCheese

Happily ever after

'This has been the most effective strategy I have tried that had an impact on support and engagement at home.'

The 'happily ever after' strategy encourages mindful gratitude that spreads to the home environment, leading to better school–home relationships.

Children enjoy having attention from their parents, and parents feel guilty about the short amounts of time they have available for their children, due to life commitments. Children will say whatever they can to get attention from the adults in their lives. This strategy develops the positivity in a child's life, leading to generally happier school and home-life situations.

- To begin, explain to children what is happening. Discuss all the good things that have happened in the day and how it makes us feel good when we remember them. Then explain that parents like to hear about the good things and how their children are enjoying their day at school.
- In the last few minutes of the school day, have each child take a few mindful belly breaths as they identify at least one thing that was very good about the day. You may want to get all children to verbalise their positive memory or call on a few different children. Some children may find this difficult at first, especially if they tend to focus on the negative.
- Instruct the children that the first thing they should tell their parent when they see them is that positive memory. Explain that it is okay for them to tell their parents anything that upsets them during the day, but they should always start with the positive.

Teaching tip

Encourage parents to always ask children about what GOOD things have happened today and then encourage discussion around why that was a good thing and how it made them feel. For the majority of children, regular, minor childhood annoyances will start to become insignificant and their attitudes towards the good things in life will blossom, as the positivity filters into their home lives and receives the majority of the parental attention.

#HappilyEverAfter

Gratitude diary

'Being thoughtful about different things made the children feel calm, happy, upbeat, communicative, smiley and positive.'

Positive communication between home and school is important for both parents and teachers. This mindful strategy keeps the lines of communication open through a child's own words. It allows mindfulness to be brought home by encouraging positive conversations between the child and parents.

Teaching tip

If access to notebooks is difficult, create a sheet that goes home each week with space for the child and parent to write. Keep all returned sheets in a file and, at the end of each term or the year, bind them together in a book to send home.

- Give each child a small notebook and have them decorate the front cover with pictures and words that express what they are grateful for in their lives.
- On the inside of the front cover, glue in a simple message to parents, explaining what its purpose is and how they can interact with their child in the diary. Encourage parents to write in the diaries and to have conversations with their child about the things they are grateful for in their lives.
- At the end of designated days, set the mindful mood by having children close their eyes, take a few deep, mindful belly breaths and consider what good things have happened during the day.
- Ask the child to date the page and then write in their diary at least one thing they were grateful/thankful for during the day. It can be a sentence or two, or even a picture. This is THEIR diary.
- Allow children to share their work if they choose, discussing their feelings and those of others (see Part 6: Emotional intelligence).
- The children should take their diary home and share it with their parents. Parents can then write in their own moments of gratitude, as explained inside the diary cover. The diary should be returned the next day.

#GratitudeDiary

Gratitude jar

'This positive habit is addictive.'

The gratitude jar is a visual reminder to focus on the positives of the day rather than wallowing in the negatives.

As humans, we tend to default to all things negative. The negative thought processes begin as an endless loop of only seeing the things that go wrong, no matter how small they really are. By practising mindfulness, we begin to develop new habits that focus on the positives in life, changing the default to positive thoughts.

- You will need a LARGE jar and lots of small paper slips.
- Determine the length of time you will spend filling the jar – a week, month, term or year. Whatever length of time you use, ensure you continue for that time period. It needs to become a habit.
- Take time to discuss what it means to show gratitude or be thankful. Allow children to discuss their feelings and how others may feel about the same situations.
- Each week, have each child write the date and one thing they are grateful for during that week, fold the paper and put it in the jar.
- If, during the week, a child expresses gratitude without prompting, encourage them to write it on a note and put it in the jar.
- At the end of the designated time, take out all of the notes and share them with the class. Count them, read them and discuss them. Talk about what has been the number one thing they have been grateful for and how their attitudes towards gratitude and being thankful have changed.

Teaching tip

Have a jar for each child in the class and allow them to fill up their own jars over the time frame, before taking them home to share with their families.

Taking it further

Challenge families to have their own gratitude jar at home, allowing the child to be the model of mindfulness and encouraging the sharing of a positive life skill.

#GratitudeJar

Mindful verbal feedback

'This is a mindful and effective way to feed back to children.'

Verbal feedback can actively support the progress of children in their learning. However, the style and manner in which the feedback is given is very important in order for it to have the intended outcome.

When we consider that our brains tend to lead down paths of negativity, it will be no surprise to a teacher when, despite outlining what a child has done correctly in their work, the child focuses on what the teacher said needs to be improved. They are unable to identify the positives that the teacher wants them to continue to do in their work. As teachers, we need to be mindful of this and be explicit in our feedback to children. This explicit, positive feedback will support your class's on-going mindfulness development.

- Prepare the children with a discussion about verbal feedback, what it is for and how it will help their learning and progress. Discuss with the children what a compliment is and how compliments are supposed to make us feel. Identify the emotions and gratitude.
- When giving the child verbal feedback, start with 'I want to give you a compliment/compliments', followed by the positive aspects of their work.
- Allow this to be taken in and for the child to realise that you are grateful for what they have done correctly.
- Children will start remembering the compliments as they are valued and repeated in more work.

#MindfulVerbalFeedback

Week of gratitude

'This feeds into a more positive working environment, allowing the children to work well in groups.'

This strategy allows children to explore the different aspects of gratitude.

Life is made of up good and bad things. Supporting and encouraging the development of the 'bright side of life' gives us the ability to evaluate life with more balance.

- Determine how the children will record their week. Some ideas are:
  - a simple table divided into five squares
  - a large flower with five petals
  - a bullseye/target
  - a small booklet.
- The week before, document and discuss with children:
  - What does gratitude mean?
  - When do we feel gratitude?
  - What is that feeling or feelings?
  - How does it make others feel?
- Each day, give the class five to ten minutes to write and/or draw, according to the theme:
  - **Memory Monday:** Describe a happy/good memory.
  - **Thoughtful Tuesday:** How have others been helpful to you?
  - **Whimsical Wednesday:** Describe a fun or funny memory.
  - **Thankful Thursday:** What are they thankful for in their life?
  - **Family Friday:** Describe what is good and special about their family.
- At the end of the week, share, discuss and explain their work. Discuss the questions explored before the week's activities. How do they compare? Has their understanding of gratitude changed or grown? How? Why?

Teaching tip

This is a good activity to use in the run-up to holiday seasons or events, in order to support the meaningful quality of these special events.

Taking it further

Involve families by encouraging discussion at home the day before or on the day, to support the development of mindful gratitude beyond the classroom.

#WeekOfGratitude

Themed appreciation weeks

'The children have become more thoughtful and thankful for the people in their lives.'

Our lives would be more difficult at this present moment if certain people were not there. Themed appreciation weeks allow our class or school to focus on these important people in our lives.

Determine the number of weeks you would like to dedicate to this mindful strategy and, working with your class, identify important people in their lives whom they could celebrate and appreciate. Then plan out the weeks together. Examples are:

- teachers
- teaching assistants
- head teacher/deputy head teacher, etc.
- office workers
- kitchen staff
- neighbours
- grandparents
- friends.

During the week, devote time to learning about these people, invite them to class, have the children ask them questions and allow the children to discuss the importance of these people in their lives.

Children can then promote the appreciation of these people by doing one of the following:

- Send thank you cards.
- Put up thank you posters around the school, home and community.
- Write about these people and put it on the school's website, blog, Twitter or Facebook account.
- Allow children to come up with their own ideas.

Teaching tip

Use the word 'appreciation' frequently in class, even when speaking of other things, and have the children use the word when they speak and write. Being explicit about our appreciation makes it normal and natural for children.

Taking it further

Keep a class diary of the appreciation week's activities, allowing children to include their thoughts and messages of thanks, or make a growing display that keeps the idea of appreciation fresh.

#AppreciationWeek

Fab five

'This is brilliant to use when working with anxious or distressed children to help them embrace positivity in their lives.'

'Fab five' encourages thought around the good things happening in our lives and enjoying those precious moments of gratitude.

Gratitude is a fundamental component of mindfulness. Teaching children (and adults) to be thankful for the abundance in their lives, as opposed to focusing on material objects, is not always readily accepted in our society.

Materials required:
- plain paper
- markers, coloured pencil or crayons.

How to:
- Take some time to discuss with the class what fabulous things they are thankful for having in their lives. Don't allow them to only focus on material things. Encourage non-tangible things as well, such as love from an individual, time spent with someone special or a friendship. Discuss why they are thankful for these things.
- Have each child place their hand on a sheet of plain paper with their fingers spread, and trace around their hand (it doesn't matter which hand).
- Then, in each finger, have them write and/or draw one thing they are thankful for having in their lives. In the end, they will have five fabulous things that they are thankful for.
- In the palm, children should either draw something that represents their personality or write their name.
- Place the completed drawings somewhere they can always see them. Encourage children to look at them often during the day as a reminder to be thankful.

Bonus idea ★

Have the children create a new hand each month, so that you can create a book for the end of the year for them to take home as a reminder of the fab year they had in your class!

#FabFive

Thankful wall

'This is our favourite display in the classroom!'

A 'thankful wall' documents the growth of mindful gratitude and promotes the cycle of positivity.

People who show greater gratitude are able to develop more friendships and have better physical and psychological health. It also enhances empathy and reduces aggression. Teaching children how to be thankful and celebrating thankfulness can support overall mindfulness development, leading to a happier, calmer class.

- Dedicate space for your 'thankful wall' at the beginning of the year.
- Decorate this space according to your class theme or as a barren tree (only trunk and limbs).
- Ensure you have a good selection of leaves or other appropriate shapes large enough for the children to write on throughout the year. These can be pre-cut, child-made or a combination. Add appropriate seasonal decorations, e.g. bats and ghosts for Halloween, Christmas decorations, snowflakes, hearts, Easter eggs, etc.
- Start the thankful wall with a discussion about what we are thankful for in our lives and have children fill in one shape with their name and date. Encourage the children to verbally share what they have written as they put it on the display.
- During a dedicated time every week, have each child write a new thankful message to share and put on the display.
- Encourage spontaneous thankfulness and allow children to put a thankful message on the display whenever they feel the desire.

#ThankfulWall

#PositivePostItDay

'It is the best day EVER! It really changed the attitude of the class and school.'

#PositivePostItDay was started by a young lady in Canada called Caitlin Haacke. After being bullied herself, she decided to take a stand against bullying. She single-handedly started this movement of positivity that is sweeping the world.

Gratitude is an emotional state of mind. To be gracious means to have an attitude towards life that gives us, as humans, a sense of rational and personal well-being. It is a strong, feel-good emotion that releases endorphins, relaxing the body and making us feel happy. This is why positivity begets positivity – it is ADDICTIVE!

The idea is simple and takes a minimum amount of planning and execution.

- Decide on the day that you will declare as #PositivePostItDay, either as a class, a group of classes or as a school. Share this with children, staff and parents.
- Prepare for the day by ensuring you have A LOT of Post-it notes. They can be any size, shape or colour.
- On the day, discuss what we like in other people and in ourselves and then have children write **at least** two positive notes, one to themselves and one to someone else.
- Allow the children to stick the notes EVERYWHERE: on a person, on a door, on a table, on a wall, etc. Fill your classroom, area or school with these little positive notes.
- At the end of the day, have the children discuss how being positive affected them. Was it difficult to think of something positive about another person? Was it difficult to think of something positive about themselves?

Taking it further

Get parents involved by ensuring they have access to Post-it notes, and encourage them to write positive messages to share. If your school has a social media site, website or blog, take lots of pictures and get them uploaded to share with the world. Make sure you tag them as #PositivePostItDay.

#PositivePostItDay

Yoga

Part 5

Pose of the week

'The children enjoy the calming effects of yoga poses.'

Yoga is one way of practising mindfulness as it helps children to reconnect with their bodies.

Each week, choose a different yoga pose. Some of the best poses to teach children in the beginning, and which they will find fun, are:

- Tree
- Mountain
- Child
- Cow
- Cat
- Downward dog
- Plank
- Star
- Dolphin
- Warrior 1, Warrior 2 and Warrior 3 (aeroplane).

The following website provides visual examples of these poses: https://educationsvoice.files.wordpress.com/2016/02/yoga-poses-that-support-mindfulness-wp.pdf

Teach the children the new pose via either a video or a picture. Model the pose and reinforce that the poses do not need to be perfect. However, they do require a focus on the bodily sensations in the moment.

While children are focusing on the sensations in their body, have them breathe deeply and allow themselves to be in the pose.

Bonus idea ★

After several weeks of different poses, make one of the days a 'mix it up day' and allow the children to choose their own pose from the poses they've learnt.

Taking it further

Choose various times in the day for the children to all get into the pose of the week. For example during transition times (the beginning or end of a lesson, transitioning between activities, the start or the end of the day), or when the children are getting restless, ring a bell or other chosen sound to signal a mindful break with a yoga pose.

#PoseOfTheWeek

Yoga trivia

'The game quality of this idea captures their imagination and has children really considering yoga poses.'

This creative and active game gets children mindfully thinking, listening and participating in an exciting and different way.

'Yoga trivia' focuses on enhancing some of the benefits of yoga, particularly improving self-confidence and self-esteem while enhancing organisational and communication skills.

- Have either a poster with yoga poses or a deck of yoga cards available to be used by the game leader.
- The leader gives clues to a yoga pose they want the others to perform without naming the pose. Example:
  - Clue 1: This pose will stretch your back.
  - Clue 2: This pose requires you to have both your hands and knees on the floor.
  - Clue 3: This pose is done by arching your back upwards.
  - Answer: Cat pose.
- The players should listen mindfully to the clues and get into the pose that they believe is being described in as few clues as possible, but without shouting out the name of the pose.
- Continue the game by having the children take turns being the leader and giving clues to a chosen yoga pose.
- Remind children to focus on their breathing and the sensations of their body once they have moved into the pose.

Teaching tip

It is best for the teacher to model the game for the first time, with the teacher remaining the leader so that children get a firm grasp of how to give clues.

Taking it further

Incorporate writing skills by having each child choose three different yoga poses and writing out the clues before the game begins.

#YogaTrivia

Sun salutation

'Once they knew the individual poses and practised the routine a few times, the children were begging to do this at the beginning of each day.'

The sun salutation is a series of poses performed in a single flow. The coordination of the breath with each move in the pose supports the movements and enhances the mindfulness effects.

The sun salutation builds strength and increases flexibility. There are different styles of performing the sun salutation. This is a beginner's routine, which can support you and your class on the road to mindfulness.

Before beginning, consider how much room is required for all of the movements without children invading each other's personal yoga space.

- Begin in the **mountain pose**, by standing with feet together, toes pointing forward and arms at your side. Hold for three deep breaths.
- Extend the **mountain pose** by inhaling and raising your arms over your head.
- Complete the **forward bend pose** by exhaling as you bend forward from the hips. You can bend your knees until your fingertips touch the floor.
- Next, go into the **kneeling lunge pose** by inhaling, keeping your right foot between your hands and stretching your left leg behind you. Shift your body forward until your right knee is fully bent at a right angle. Make sure you keep your palms on the floor and allow your head to hang forward.

- Exhale and go into a **plank pose**. Bring your right knee back to straighten the leg. Arms need to be straight with palms on the floor. Hold your body in a straight line.
- Inhale and go into a **cat pose**, with your hands directly under your shoulders and your knees on the floor, arching your back.
- Exhale and lower yourself into the **child pose**, kneeling down and leaning forward with your arms outstretched in front of you.
- Inhale and come up into the **cobra pose** by raising your upper body, keeping your elbows bent and your shoulders away from your ears.
- Exhale and go into the **downward dog pose**, with your weight on your hands and feet and your bottom in the air, in an upside-down 'V' shape.
- Inhale and go into a **kneeling lunge pose**, with your right foot between your hands, and shift forward until your right knee is fully bent again.
- Exhale and bring your left foot up beside your right foot and go into a **forward bend pose** again.
- Inhale, raise your hands above your head and into an **extended mountain pose**.
- Hold for several breaths and then repeat, using the opposite foot as the lead.

Taking it further

Once the children become 'experts', have them lead a playtime or lunchtime yoga club, using the sun salutation as the basis for their activities.

#SunSalutation

Body part yoga game

'This is a clever way to get children using yoga, particularly those that are more reluctant.'

This fun yoga game allows children to stretch, balance and concentrate only on the present moment.

Taking it further

Spice up the game by pulling two or more cards from the deck at a time or starting with one card, finding a pose, adding a second card, finding another pose, adding a third card and making the final pose using all three body parts.

The cultivation of focused attention supports the development of being in the present moment and being mindfully aware. Being mindfully aware is different from just the everyday notion of paying attention. Mindful awareness is about sensing and observing the internal sensations.

The goal of this game is to create a yoga pose that includes the use of the identified body part TOUCHING the ground.

- Create several simple sets of cards that include body parts: head, foot, both feet, hand, both hands, elbow, both elbows, knee, both knees, bottom, back, stomach, etc. (Include any body parts that are appropriate for your class.)
- Divide the children into pairs, small groups or a whole class.
- The leader draws one card from the deck of cards and reads it out.
- The rest of the children create a yoga pose (real or made up) that includes that body part being on the ground/floor and hold it for three deep breaths, focusing on the breath and sensations of the body.
- Repeat for the length of time desired.

#BodyPartYoga

Themed yoga

'This is one of the highlights of our topic work! The connections children are making, both mindfully and academically, make this one of my go-to ideas.'

Themes add context and variety to yoga while also supporting the development of the topics of learning.

Who doesn't like a good thematic unit?

Of course, there are proper names for yoga poses. However, when using yoga to develop mindfulness in the young, it is more important to get them happily involved with strategy than with specific names.

Thematic yoga is simple. All you need is the topic you have decided to work on in class – this could be anything from the farm to outer space. Then get the class's creative juices flowing!

- Identify the key vocabulary in the topic that you want the children to learn and understand.
- As you teach each new word, have the children explore how that word could be translated into a yoga pose and why. You want the children to attach meaning to a physical and mental state.
- As a class, decide on the yoga pose to use, take a picture and add it to your display board next to the vocabulary.
- Now that you have a new set of yoga poses, create your own poster or cards.

Children will show lots of creativity as they attach meaning to the poses, supporting not only their mental well-being but also their academic development.

Teaching tip

In the beginning, the children will be caught up in the excitement of creating or renaming the yoga poses. Allow them that excitement, punctuated with breathing exercises to calm them down, and remind them to focus on the breath and sensations of the body when in the poses. This allows the mind to calm and the body to relax.

Bonus idea ★

Take the new yoga poses into PE as part of Idea 47: Warm up/cool down, out on the playground as part of Idea 46: Yogi says, or incorporate them in Idea 44: Tell a story yoga.

#ThemedYoga

Tell a story yoga

'This body-centred activity not only supports mindfulness development and enhancement, but also allows for the development of oral and literacy skills.'

The developing of new storylines or the simple retelling of a story through yoga poses combines movement with the spoken word, actively increases the neural connections by multiple stimuli, and brings a story to life in a mindfully considered way.

Choose a story that is relevant to your class, either oral or in book-form, to tell/read to the children. It can be a traditional fairy tale, a thematic-based story or simply one that you know your class will enjoy. There is no right or wrong. However, ensure that the story is not too long as you need to consider the time it will take when you combine it with yoga. Also, consider the space you will need for this activity.

Explain to the children that you are going to tell/read them a story and you want them to consider mindfully each part of the story. Continue to explain that you will stop at various points in the story and it is at these points that they are to do a yoga pose that re-enacts that section. They are to hold that pose, breathing deeply and mindfully listening to the story, until you stop and they take up a new pose.

Begin with all the children standing in mountain pose and start the tale. Let the story unfold!

Taking it further

Divide children into small groups and allow them to use their imaginations to create their own stories, using yoga poses to act out the plot. Continue to capitalise on this mindful activity by then using it as a springboard for writing the story in class.

Bonus idea ★

For pre or early writers/readers, develop comprehension skills by encouraging them to verbally retell the story, incorporating yoga poses.

#TellAStoryYoga

Yoga charades

'Spelling has never been so exciting!'

This is a twist on the traditional game of charades, which gets children mindfully considering their body movements while challenging others to identify a word spelled.

Identifying the sensations of the body along with the concepts being taught allows for more depth in the connections in the learning. When doing yoga with a partner, children learn to appreciate what they can achieve when they focus on supporting one another.

- Create a set of word cards that are significant for your class. They could be high frequency words, a spelling list, subject vocabulary words or commonly misspelled words. Make it personal to your class.
- Divide the class into groups of three to five children.
- Give each group a word card and give them five minutes to consider how they can pose their bodies, one letter at a time, to spell out the given word.
- Then, let the game begin!
- Give each child a whiteboard to use during the game.
- Ask each group to get into the pose for each letter of their word, holding the pose for five deep breaths.
- The other children should write the letters they see, without shouting out, until they have a word.
- When the group is finished, they should show the class their word and read it out. If a child gets it correct, they get a point. (Allow them to keep a tally on their whiteboards.)

Teaching tip

When beginning to use this activity, allow time for the children to explore how to form letters with their bodies as a team. Challenge the children to form the letters only in upright poses and not laying on the floor.

Bonus idea ★

For the younger children who are just learning their letters and sounds, have them work in pairs or groups of three to come up with a pose for the new letter/sound/phoneme being learned. Have the children get into the pose, inhaling and exhaling using the sound it makes.

#YogaCharades

Yogi says

'It is the new favourite game on the playground.'

'Yogi says' is yoga with a twist on the traditional game 'Simon says'. It is simple and can be done just about anywhere you want, even in the playground at break times!

Actively engaging children in mindfulness on a daily basis is important. Opportunities to develop mindfulness skills and strategies will strengthen their ability to be mindful more often and see it as part of their lifestyle, rather than something they have to think about. It needs to become a habit for it to be most useful and successful. Yoga is known to actively enhance the mind and body connection.

- You will need three or more players.
- One player should be designated as the yogi.
- The yogi will then issue instructions to the other players about which yoga pose to perform, which should only be followed if the yogi says, 'Yogi says. . .' (Example: 'Yogi says to do the mountain pose.')
- The yogi ALWAYS does the pose, no matter what the instruction given.
- Players are encouraged to use their mindful listening skills to listen to the instructions.
- Should a player complete the yoga pose without 'Yogi says. . .' being used in the instruction, they are out of the game.
- The game continues until there is only one player left. They now become the yogi and the game repeats.

Players should be reminded to focus on listening to the instructions, their breathing and the sensations the body makes when completing a pose.

#YogiSays

Warm up/cool down

'The calming effects of the yoga routines are always a sure way to begin and end PE lessons on a positive note.'

Using yoga to warm up and cool down will help children to slow down, chill out, relax their minds and exercise their bodies.

Yoga lowers the heart rate and supports self-discipline development and control. In this time, children practice the self-regulation of breathing that is a natural relaxation response in humans, allowing for a calmer transition to an active PE lesson, as well as a calmer transition back into classroom lessons.

You will need to teach your children a number of yoga poses. You can do this after a number of weeks practising Idea 39: Pose of the week, or you can spend a few PE lessons focusing on the yoga poses.

Decide on a routine that uses five to eight of your class's favourite poses to start and end your PE sessions.

Some good yoga poses to use with the children for this activity are:
- Mountain
- Downward dog
- Cat to cow
- Butterfly
- Child
- Eagle arms
- Bridge
- Eye of the needle
- Plank
- Corpse pose, with a one-minute breathing meditation (particularly as the end of the cool-down routine).

Then, make it a habit! No matter what, start and end your PE sessions with yoga.

> **Teaching tip**
>
> Model and remind children about focusing on breathing and the sensations of the body. A quick Idea 8: Body scan meditation during the training of yoga poses will ensure that the children are being mindful.

> **Bonus idea** ★
>
> After the children have become successful at using yoga as a part of their PE lesson, have them develop their own routines and allow them to lead these PE sessions to encourage independence in yoga and mindfulness practice.

#WarmUpAndCoolDown

Emotional
Intelligence

Part 6

Emotion talk

'This changed the atmosphere of my classroom.'

The first step in developing emotional intelligence is to get children to understand that their emotions are valid. It is okay to have emotions, good or bad. It is how we deal with and react to these emotions that makes a difference.

We need to talk about emotions often and every day, as part of our daily practice. If you are not used to talking about emotions, this can be difficult. However, the more you do it, the better you will get at doing it, and your class will follow your lead.

Begin by identifying the emotions felt during a day. Usually, children will only identify a few basic emotions such as happy, sad, mad and scared. However, ensure that other emotions are identified: calm, mischievous, confused, exhausted, optimistic, frustrated, frightened, jealous, shy, shocked, guilty, etc.

- How does each emotion feel? Is it a good emotion to have? Explain. How can you change that emotion? (Encourage the use of mindfulness strategies.)
- Begin the day with each child telling you and the class how they feel and why. 'Today I am feeling confident because I practised my maths last night.'
- In the heat of the moment, good or bad, ask the child, 'What emotion are you feeling right now?' If they have a problem identifying the emotion, then say, 'I can see that you are feeling. . . because. . .'
- Explain your own emotions to children and what you can do to change them. 'Miss Smith is feeling frustrated by children not mindfully listening. So, I need a mindful moment and we all need to take ten snake breaths.'

#EmotionTalk

Read all about it!

'It helps to develop their critical thinking skills and empathy.'

Guided reading sessions are excellent for the development of mindfulness, as higher order thinking questions force children to explore characters more deeply.

Mindfulness includes being aware of the emotions floating around us that are coming from other people and how they make us feel. Recognising these can be more difficult for children and requires more time and practice to develop.

Emotional intelligence:
- How is the character feeling at this moment?
- How does this emotion affect what is happening in the story right now? How do you think it will affect the story later on?
- How do you think this character's emotions are affecting the other characters? Explain how we know this.
- How are this character's emotions making you feel? Explain.

Present moment:
- Does the character realise and appreciate what is happening at this very moment? Explain why you think the character is or is not appreciating the present moment.
- How would it be different if you were this character? Explain.

Dialogue:
- When the character is speaking, are they being mindful in what they are saying? Are the words considered true, kind or helpful? Explain why or why not.
- What impact is this dialogue having on the story and the other characters? Explain.
- If you were the character, what would you say? Why would you say that?

Teaching tip

When asking the questions, ensure that you challenge the children's thinking, as appropriate for their age group. Get them thinking past the superficial and exploring the meaning of the words, and how the author has crafted them to elicit emotions from the characters. Compare how this fits with their own personal mindfulness.

#ReadAllAboutIt

Emotions card games

'I am impressed by how quickly the children have begun to understand the different emotions and support each other with their emotions.'

Using emotion cards and games will support the mindfulness development of emotional intelligence by getting children to recognise their emotions.

Teaching tip

Younger children tend to discuss their emotions more openly. Older children are sometimes more timid. Take the time to allow older children to become comfortable and use yourself as a good role model by talking about your own emotions.

Many children do not understand and/or display appropriate emotions in themselves or identify appropriate emotions in others. The misunderstanding of facial expressions, body language, verbal intonations and reactions can lead to inappropriate responses, such as arguments, upset and sometimes physical altercations.

You will need to create flashcards using **real** pictures of people's faces displaying a variety of emotions. The pictures can be some that you have copied from other sources or they can be made with the children in your class. It is important that the faces are real. Put the name of the emotion underneath the picture.

Emotional charades:
Shuffle the cards and lay them face down. The first player picks a card and does not show it to anyone else. They should then mimic the face they see on the card while using other non-verbal and verbal reactions, WITHOUT saying the emotion. The other players guess the emotion. The winner gets to select the next card.

'The bin busted' storytelling:
Shuffle the cards and lay them face down. The first player selects a card and begins to tell a story that incorporates the emotion on the card, building the beginning of the story narrative. After about a minute, they stop the

development of the story by saying, 'and the bin busted'. This signals the next player to collect a card and continue the story, ensuring the inclusion of the emotion on the card in the narrative. Again, after a minute, they will say, 'and the bin busted'. The story continues to develop in this fashion, with an emphasis of bringing it to a conclusion with the last player. Remind children that they must always include the emotion of their card while also considering the development of the story: the beginning, middle and end. This will require lots of mindful listening and being in the present moment, as their minds will want to fast-forward to the future to decide what they will be saying for their part.

I can explain:

Shuffle the cards and lay them face down. Each player will take it in turns to select a card. Without showing the card to the others and without saying what emotion is on the card, they are to explain to the other children what emotion card they are holding. The first child to guess the correct emotion gets the card. After all the cards are explained, the player with the most cards wins the game. This game is best played in groups of three to five.

Taking it further

After the children have mastered their understanding of emotions, explanation of emotions and these games, have them buddy up with a group in another class that has never played the game before. They should explain the game and support the group as they learn how to talk about emotions.

#EmotionsCardGames

A very emotional day

'A class favourite! It is the most read story in the class library.'

'A very emotional day' is a class writing activity that allows children to explore individual emotions, but also look at how a person can have many emotions in a day, how they can use mindfulness to support those emotions and how to find the balance at the end.

You will use the emotions flash cards from Idea 50 as a springboard for the writing.

- Before you begin, explain to the class that they will be working together to write a class story called 'A very emotional day'. The plot of the story involves the character having lots of different emotions during the day and the key is how they are able to use mindfulness to support that emotion.
- Together, decide on the basics of the story – character and setting – and write the first paragraph.
- Place the cards face down and have each child/pair select a card. Allow time for children to discuss with partners which emotion they have and what they will write in their paragraph.
- Each child or pair now writes one paragraph in this story. The paragraph needs to explain what is happening to the character, how they are feeling and how they are reacting to this emotion using mindfulness.
- Once all the paragraphs have been written, bring them together as one story to read to the class.
- Allow the children to discuss the story, how the day went and how the character may be feeling at the end of such an eventful day.
- Conclude the story as a class by writing the last paragraph.
- Publish and share with others!

#AVeryEmotionalDay

Mindful sensory poetry

'Children have been noticing things they have never noticed before.'

Sensory poetry is a fun and easy way to incorporate the development of mindfulness into the curriculum. It doesn't rely on rhyme, but on the description of the five senses: sight, smell, touch, taste and hearing. Mindful sensory poetry adds one more dimension: emotion.

To begin, the children need to have a real-life experience in which they can mindfully explore these six aspects. A theme that lends itself well to this type of poetry and activity is the different seasons of the year. This can be done by:

- Taking a basic mindful walk (see Idea 88). During this walk, stop the children to consider each of the six aspects of the poem. They can write down their thoughts on their clipboards/notepads/whiteboards.
- Participating in a five-minute guided meditation (see Part 2). Guide the children through a five-minute deep breathing meditation, softly encouraging them to be present in the moment and identify each of the aspects they will be writing about in the poem individually. Following the meditation, have them write down their thoughts.

Children then need time to develop the thoughts that will be used in the poem. Give them time to discuss each of the six aspects they encountered during their experience, supporting the development of vocabulary and writing skills.

Once the children have explored their thoughts and feelings, have them write their poem, ensuring that all six aspects are included in their final poem.

Teaching tip

Give the poetry purpose and 'publish' it, to share with other classes as a springboard for their own discussion and mindfulness development.

Taking it further

Explore how different colours make you feel and what sensations you have when seeing specific colours. What colours can children 'feel' in their poem? What sensations does the poem convey? Have children illustrate their poem using colours and Idea 62: Basic mindful doodling.

#MindfulSensoryPoetry

65

Mantras

'You can feel the positivity in the room. It brings a sense of purpose and happiness every time we repeat our class mantra.'

Paying attention is an important part of mindfulness. Being positive within that attention has a lasting impact on our overall well-being. A mantra is a word or phrase repeated over and over, and helps keep us focused during times of mindfulness while also affirming one's worth and desires.

When beginning to use mantras, a clear discussion about what they are and why we use them will support a child's independent emotional development and thoughts on using them in the future.

- Ask individuals to come up with their own yearly, monthly, weekly or daily mantras. The only criterion is that they must be positive in nature. Examples include: I am happy; I am good; Let it go; Peace; I am loved.
- Children work together to create a class list of mantras.
- While playing soft meditation music, have the children begin a simple deep-breathing meditation. On the exhale, they repeat the chosen mantra in their heads.
- Take a moment at various points during the day for children to take a few deep breaths and repeat their mantra silently in their heads before continuing their work.
- Create signs and posters with mantras to use around the classroom and/or around the school, to serve as reminders and encourage positive mindful moments.

Taking it further

As part of a home learning assignment, have children spend a few minutes with their families coming up with their own family mantras and ideas on how they can use them to become more mindful as a family. Leave the project open-ended but you may need to encourage children with ideas on how they can be used in the home. Allow children to share their experiences with the class as appropriate.

#Mantras

Mindful stones

'Without any prompting, I am seeing the children rub their special stone and repeating the words they have chosen. It really works to calm them down!'

Children can easily get lost in a day with the pace of lessons, new learning, changes in friendships, transition times and more. Mindful stones are tangible objects to use as a mindful focus, reminding children of the skills they are learning so that they don't need to be verbally reminded.

Mindful stones can be created as follows.

Materials:
- one stone per child
- old magazines
- PVA glue
- small paint brushes.

Instructions:
- Look for words in the magazines that are positive in nature and mean something to the individual (great, good, cool, positive, strong, brave, etc.).
- Cut out the words and glue them to the stone. (Words need to be small in size so that children can get several words on their stone.)
- Repeat until the stone is completely covered in positive words and/or phrases.
- Completely cover the finished stone in glue and allow it to dry.

Ideas on how to use mindful stones:
- Allow each child to keep their stone at their seat and tell them that when they are feeling upset, worried, frustrated, etc., they should rub the stone, reading the words and taking deep, mindful breaths. Once calm, they can continue their work.
- Use the stones as a focus point during class or group meditations.

Bonus idea ★

Allow children to use their artistic skills to create their mindful stone, using paints or permanent markers to decorate the stone with mantras, patterns or both, before sealing it with PVA glue.

Taking it further

Collect the stones and share them randomly each week so that the children can also be inspired by what others created.

#MindfulStones

RAIN

'The change in the class atmosphere is immediate.'

RAIN is an acronym that provides an easy strategy to develop mindfulness as a lifelong skill. It is a tool for self-compassion that enhances awareness and curiosity rather than reaction.

R – Recognise what's going on around you. Recognise the thoughts, feelings and behaviours that are making you feel the way you do.

A – Allow the experience to be just as it is. Allow it by stopping and relaxing. Let the experience just be as it is.

I – Investigate with kindness. Pause and ask what is happening inside yourself.

N – Natural, LOVING kindness towards yourself! Give yourself a hug and tell yourself that you are a good, kind and caring person.

When teaching children this strategy:

- In the beginning, take time to discuss each letter, what it means and how we can do this. Allow children to explore their thoughts, particularly how they affect them emotionally.
- Agree on a time/moment that, as a class, they will use RAIN and a signal that will start the use of the strategy. This could be during transition periods, independent work or active learning. There is no right or wrong time.
- Guide the children through the acronym (this should take less than 30 seconds in total).
- Over time, encourage the children to recognise opportunities when they can use RAIN independently in order to calm themselves down and take control of their emotions.

#RAIN

Body writing

'The deep concentration and focus makes for a relaxing and beneficial spelling and mindfulness session.'

The sense of touch allows for focused awareness of the moment through a non-verbal experience. The sense of touch itself provides contact and warmth, associated with many positive emotions and feelings. With body writing, the focus is clearly defined and deep concentration is required.

- Divide the children into pairs. Explain to the children that they must work quietly as they will have to concentrate on the writing on their back. Taking deep breaths will help to calm and focus them on the moment.
- Child A sits with his/her back to the other. The writer, Child B, uses their index finger to write on Child A's back.
- Once Child B is finished writing, they are to signal Child A by placing a hand lightly on their shoulder.
- At this point, Child A makes a guess at what is written on their back.
- If it is correct, Child B says 'Yes' and they switch positions and change roles.
- If it is not correct, Child B says 'No' and writes it again. If they are incorrect three times, they swap roles.
- Using softly playing meditation music in the background will create an atmosphere that will support the success of this strategy.

Teaching tip

Before beginning, set rules for the body writing, explaining that the acceptable areas for writing are within a specific area of the back. The child writing should not be speaking and should only confirm whether the other individual has guessed what has been written.

Taking it further

For younger children, this can be part of the process of learning how to write and identify letters and sounds. As they get older, you can use it as part of their spelling lessons with their spelling lists. More mature children can create positive affirmations and mantras to use.

#FingertipWriting

Song shuffle

'I was surprised by the differences in emotions that the children felt from the same piece of music. Eye-opening!'

Music has its own language and emotions. 'Song shuffle' is a way to explore these different emotions so that we can better understand them in our everyday lives.

To prepare:

Compile a playlist of short pieces of songs (30 seconds) from a variety of genres and artists. You will want to consider how the music makes you feel so that you can ensure there is a good mix of emotions. Some may have words and some may be just instrumental.

How to:

- Have children identify what they enjoy in music and what their favourite songs are and why. Discuss how different songs can make you feel. Explain that they will explore emotions through a series of musical selections. As you play each snippet, they should consider the following:
  - What sensations are you feeling in your body?
  - What does the song remind you of or what images come to your mind as you listen?
  - What emotion is it making you feel and why?
- To begin, have the children sit up or lie on the floor comfortably and close their eyes. They should take three deep belly breaths, allowing their bodies to relax.
- Play the first selection. Stop the music and ask the questions you wanted children to focus on.
- Repeat with each new selection piece.
- Conclude the session by discussing what children felt and whether there were any patterns to the emotions they had.

#SongShuffle

Inside Out – the film

'This was a great way to open up discussion and understanding about emotions.'

Inside Out is an animated film about the five core emotions: anger, disgust, fear, sadness and joy. It encourages us to get to know our emotions and how we process those emotions.

Emotional intelligence is the capacity of individuals to recognise their own and other people's emotions, to discriminate between different feelings and label them appropriately, and to use emotional information to guide thinking and behaviour. It is about naming our feelings and understanding why we have those feelings.

- Use the film as a basis for understanding the science behind emotions.
- Discuss how emotions stimulate other emotions and why.
- Role-play scenes in the film, with the children acting out how they can mindfully take control of those emotions.
- Use clips from the film to stimulate discussions with partners or small groups about what is happening in the scenes and why, ensuring the use of emotional vocabulary and considering how children could change the emotions being played out.
- Use clips from the film to stimulate writing activities around individual emotions and memories, how they make you feel and what you can do to change those emotions.

Teaching tip

When working with emotions, you know your class best. Consider any particular issues that may arise for children regarding specific emotions. Always remember to validate the emotion as the way they feel and, if possible, explore why they have that emotion.

Taking it further

Divide the class into small groups and have them write and act out a NEW scene for the film around a NEW emotion that enters the film.

#InsideOut

Track your emotions

'This idea helped me to identify some children who were being quietly anxious.'

Self-awareness is an important part of mindfulness. If we track our emotions over a period of time, we can use this as an avenue for discussing emotions, what they mean and how they make us feel.

Taking it further

Once the children are becoming good at identifying their own emotions and why they are feeling the way they feel, divide the children into pairs and give them time to identify the emotions of the other child, encouraging them to discuss what they see that tells them about the emotions of the other person.

The identification and understanding of emotions is a very important part of mindfulness development. There are several ways that you and your class can track your emotions. Whichever way you decide on, a key is to keep a record over time that can be referred to for later discussions.

Ways to track emotions:

- **Daily/weekly chart** – This chart has each day of the week divided into specific periods of time. After each period, the child makes a note of their emotions through either a quick emoticon drawing or a few words describing how they are feeling.
- **Monthly graph chart** – Each child gets a monthly grid and emotions are tracked at the end of the day. Each emotion should have a different colour (create a key). At the end of the day, children should colour in the square with the emotion they felt most during that day.
- **Emotions diary/journal** – Give each child their own journal. At the end of the day, give the class five minutes to write or draw how they have felt during the day.

It is important that once you have children tracking their emotions, they also have time to explore and discuss the emotions they are having and why. This could happen at one specific time each week or it could be a part of the daily emotion-tracking activity.

#TrackYourEmotions

Mindful colouring and doodling

Part 7

Mandala colouring

'I could physically see the children relaxing as they began to colour. This is the first strategy I use when I want to help children to calm down.'

The act of colouring allows the brain to relax and focus on one thing: being in the moment of colouring. It allows the brain time to rest and recuperate.

Research has shown that the anxiety levels in children decrease after they have spent time colouring pattern sheets. Mindful colouring gives the child's mind time to be in a calm moment and absorb the information that it has been given.

Before you begin, ensure you have a large collection of mandala colouring sheets available to use. There are many free, printable and appropriate mandalas located on the internet.

- Have a set time every day with ten to 15 minutes devoted to mindful colouring. This is particularly useful at the end of the day or between transition times.
- Allow and/or plan for mindful colouring following a particularly difficult lesson, to allow time for the brain to accept the new information.
- Keep a collection of different sheets in a special mindfulness area of the classroom, to be used by children when they are feeling upset, anxious or stressed.
- When having to deal with a particularly distressed child or situation, allow the child to mindfully colour until you see them calming down before dealing with what is happening.

Teaching tip

The use of softly playing meditation music and encouraging deep, mindful breathing will support the effects of this mindfulness strategy. Encourage the children to focus on the repetitive patterns that can be seen on the mandala.

Taking it further

Mandalas have their own intrinsically mindful quality. However, colouring on its own can have similar benefits. Integrate colouring into your topic/subject work by using thematic and holiday colouring sheets, ensuring that the focus is on the mindfulness aspect of the colouring.

#MandalaColouring

Affirmation colouring

'After a few days, I began to hear the children supporting one another by repeating the affirmations they had been focusing on that week.'

It is believed that we have approximately 50,000 thoughts a day, and most of these are repeated thoughts with a negative focus. Repeated positive affirmations create positive changes in our overall perspective.

Affirmations can be an inspiration and develop self-belief by reinforcing the message. Combining mindful colouring with a positive affirmation supports the continued mindfulness development of focusing on the positive.

Before you begin, ensure that you have a large collection of affirmation colouring sheets available to use. There are many free, printable and appropriate affirmation colouring sheets located on the internet.

- As a class, discuss what an affirmation is and how positive affirmations support our own self-belief system.
- Allow children to select the affirmation they want to be their focus. In pairs or small groups, give them time to discuss why they selected that affirmation.
- Play meditation music softly in the background as the children begin to colour. During the session, remind children to repeat the affirmation they have selected silently to themselves as they focus on their breathing and colouring.

Teaching tip

Use affirmation colouring as part of a ten-to-15 minute meditation for the day and complete the sheet over a number of days.

Taking it further

Have children choose a new affirmation each week to focus on. Have each child collect their affirmations in their own folders, which they can go to for reflection.

#AffirmationColouring

Basic mindful doodling

'I will never look at doodling in the same light again!'

The goal of mindful doodling is to fully engage with the doodles in a meditative way. It requires slowing down, focusing on the paper and pen and doodling repeatedly with full intent. Thus, you become present in the moment.

Teaching tip

Some children may not fully understand what a doodle is and will need you to model the process of doodling or show them examples of mindful doodling from the internet. Before using this as a mindfulness strategy, allow children to explore the artistic aspect of the doodles and share their doodles with each other to see the variety that can be made.

Bonus idea ★

'Finish the picture' doodle: Sometimes, when a child is faced with a blank sheet, their mind also becomes blank, causing undue stress and anxiety. Give children a sheet with a partial doodle already there, which children can use as the basis for their doodle, allowing their lines and shapes to flow from this central point.

#MindfulDoodling

Materials required:
- small sheet of plain paper
- well-sharpened coloured pencils or fine-point felt-tip markers.

How to do basic mindful doodling:
- Play soft meditation music in the background with no talking during the time spent doodling (optional).
- Draw a freehand border around the outer edge.
- Draw straight, angled or curved lines within the border, dividing the area into smaller sections.
- Choose a corner of the border and begin doodling.
- Draw patterns along the contours of the border. Allow the pattern to reveal itself naturally; there is no right or wrong, and good drawing skills aren't required! Use simple shapes, lines, dots, squiggles and more. Shade as you desire but be mindful of and deliberate with each stroke.
- Remind children that there are NO mistakes, so no erasing is allowed. Embrace the mark you have made and use it to continue your meditative journey of mindfully doodling. This is about the process and not the end result.
- Keep going until you are finished.

Note: depending on the age of the children, you may want to do this over two periods of time, particularly if they are older and adding finer detail to their doodles.

Sand doodling

'The perfectionist children found this useful, as the finished results were not permanent but the process was still calming.'

Sand doodling enhances the doodling experience with the sensory aspect, which allows one to focus on the additional sensations of doodling.

Mindful doodling does not require artistic talent. However, it does require mindful focus, which allows for the development of self-awareness.

Mindful doodling is known to:
- focus the mind
- calm the body and mind
- relieve stress
- encourage relaxation
- increase your sense of well-being
- replace negative or bored habits
- allow you to be present and aware.

Materials required:
- a tray (at least the size of a sheet of paper) filled with sand
- your finger or a straight, fine-point stick.

How to sand doodle:
- Choose a corner of sand to start in.
- Start creating your doodle, with patterns drawn by your finger or stick. Allow the pattern to reveal itself naturally. There is no right or wrong.
- Keep going until the entire area is covered in doodles.

#SandDoodling

Black etch doodling

'Once I showed children how to do this one, they were wanting to do it every week as part of their meditation time.'

This is a process of creating the drawing surface by using crayon layers and then etching the doodle.

This mindfulness strategy should be done over two sessions, the colouring in of the sheet in the first session and the doodling in a different session. In both sessions, there should be a focus on the breath and what children are doing in the present moment.

Materials required:
- one plain white sheet of paper per child
- coloured pencils of all colours and black wax crayons
- popsicle sticks, tooth picks or paper clips (doodling tool).

How to do black etch doodling:
- Colour the paper with different pencil colours, except black. There is no set pattern for this and it can include a rainbow-effect pattern or just random sections of the sheet coloured in. The important part is that there should not be any uncoloured sections of the paper.
- Then, using the black crayon, heavily cover the entire sheet of paper with a thick layer.
- Once completed, using the doodling tool, begin the mindful doodle by scraping away the black crayon to reveal the colours underneath.

Optional: Instead of black crayon, cover the coloured sheet with black India ink and then allow to dry before doodling.

Graph paper doodling

'My class enjoy these mindful minutes of doodling. It really gives them a moment to breathe and relax before moving on with their work.'

Graph paper doodling is quick, with a small doodle a day or moment in time, and keeps mindfulness developing. It can become a type of journal of how you are feeling over a period of days, weeks or months by the use of lines and colour. The amount of time given to it is short, but the therapeutic effect can be long-lasting.

Mindful doodling does not have to take up much time. The key is to be focused on the present moment, no matter how long or short the time given.

Materials required:
- one sheet of paper, divided into a grid (the number and size of the boxes are up to you and should be age-appropriate)
- coloured pencils or fine-point markers.

How to do graph paper doodling:
- The children should take three deep, mindful breaths, allowing the mind to calm and the body to relax.
- Using a mindful bell to signal the doodling time, have the children focus on one square on their sheet on which to doodle. Remind them to focus on their breath and the lines they are drawing.
- After one minute, use the mindful bell to signal the end of the session. The children should put pencils and markers down and take three deep, mindful breaths and then continue with their day.

Taking it further

Link these doodles to your development of emotional intelligence. Once a week, have the children share their doodles in pairs or small groups, and discuss their doodles, how the doodles made them feel and whether they notice any patterns in the doodles (colours and designs) that reflect on their emotions of that day.

#GraphPaperDoodling

Emotions mandala

'Effective for those children that don't want to talk about emotions.'

Verbalising emotions can be difficult for some children. Emotions mandalas provide a non-verbal outlet to express emotions while also providing a basis for further discussions about how a child is feeling and their state of mind.

Teaching tip

Ensure that the time spent colouring is mindful in practice, with softly playing meditation music and the encouragement of mindful focus.

Taking it further

Complete several mandalas over a period of time (week, month or year) and give children the opportunity to look at the changes of their emotions over time. Discuss why their emotions may change or why they may stay the same. Are there any patterns in their emotions? Are some days or weeks better than others? Why do they think this is happening?

#EmotionsMandala

- As a class, agree and create a colour key for the most frequent emotions. Examples: red – anger; blue – sadness; yellow – happiness, etc.
- Print off a variety of simple mandalas and allow each child to select one to colour.
- Have the children take a quiet, mindful moment to consider how they are feeling today and then have them colour in the mandala according to their feelings. They are to use the colours in direct proportion to how they are feeling. If they have been happy more than they have been sad, then there would be more of the happy colour than the sad colour.
- Encourage use of colours of other emotions not identified in the class colour key to add to children's mandalas. Make sure they add it to their personal colour key.
- When the mandalas are complete, discuss their mandalas with the children and why they used the colours they have used. Get the children to explain their feelings rather than just saying that they are happy or sad.
- After the discussion, have children write about why they thought their day has these emotional colours.

Table-sized mandalas

'The children enjoy the calming effects of this cooperative mindfulness strategy. It is the hit of the unit.'

Collaborative mindful colouring can add a different twist to isolated mandala colouring and encourage mindful cooperation, which develops relationships and a calm environment.

Table ideas:
- Enlarge regular-sized colouring mandalas, making them as large as you can. They can be all the same mandala or different ones. Then cover the table with the sheets, ensuring that ALL of the areas can be coloured. This may require taping together the sheets on the back of the joined areas and not the front.
- Alternatively, cover the table with paper. This may require taping the paper on the back of the joined areas. Then draw one large mandala.

How to:
- Discuss with the children the importance of cooperation and how we can support one another in mindful ways.
- Give groups of children time to work together to colour in the large mandala by agreeing on the areas they will colour and the use of colours in the pattern. Remind them of the purpose of the finished product.

Using soft meditation music and encouraging deep, mindful breathing will support the effects of this mindfulness strategy. Also encourage children to focus on the designs of the mandala and the repetitive patterns that can be seen.

Taking it further

Use this as part of a maths activity on geometric shapes and have a group of children create a table-sized mandala using specific shapes (2-D shape templates can be used). Then have another group colour in the mandala created using a colour key, with each shape having a specific colour.

Bonus idea ★

Take the completed mandalas and use them as part of a display background or meditation focus point in the classroom.

#TableSizedMandalas

81

Calm down and relax

Part 8

Worry dolls

'Effective strategy for the quiet children in my class. They are happy to whisper their worries to their worry doll.'

Worry dolls are very small dolls that are usually used to soothe the worries of a person so they can have a restful sleep. Worry dolls can be used in school as well to help those children who are anxious.

Materials required:
- one wooden, knobbed peg/clothespin per child
- a selection of fabric scraps
- a selection of wool/yarn/string
- PVA glue
- scissors
- fine-tip markers.

How to make a worry doll:
- Select pieces of fabric and wrap the peg to create the clothes for the doll, gluing the fabric directly onto the peg.
- Select pieces of wool/yarn/string to create the hair and glue to the top of the peg.
- Using the fine-tip markers, create a face.

How to use the worry doll:
- Agree on where to keep the worry dolls. It could be in special containers on each table or in a central place in the classroom.
- When the child is anxious, worried, upset or angry, they should whisper their problem to the doll. Remind the children that once they tell their worry doll their problem for the day, they can let it go and the doll holds it for them so that they can get on with their work.

#WorryDolls

Mindful bubble blowing

'A great spring or summer day mindfulness strategy.'

Blowing bubbles is an excellent (and cheap) way to develop focus on the breath to support the calming effects of daily mindfulness.

Divide the children up into twos or threes. Have one child be the bubble blower and the others be the mindful observers.

Discuss with the children how deep, mindful breathing allows us to relax and calm ourselves down. Practice a few mindful breaths, talking children through the inhale and exhale and particularly focusing on the relaxation of the shoulders.

Bubble blower:
- Dip the bubble wand into the bubble solution.
- Take a deep breath through the nose, noticing how it feels to breathe in the air and how it sounds when you inhale.
- Exhale through the mouth, blowing as many bubbles as you can, noticing your shoulders relax.
- Repeat.

Observers:
- Sitting up straight, inhale and exhale in time with the blower, allowing your shoulders to relax.
- Focus attention on one of the bubbles, mindfully noticing the size, shape, colour and movement. Follow it until it floats far away or bursts.
- Repeat.

After a set amount of time, repeat with each person in the small group having the chance to be a bubble blower.

Teaching tip

To make 500ml of bubble solution, mix 150ml washing-up liquid, 350ml water and two teaspoons of granulated sugar together and store in a closed container. Bubble wands can be made out of straws, plastic slotted spoons, top ends of a salt shaker, pipe cleaners, etc.

#MindfulBubbleBlowing

Mindful stress ball

'Relaxing and effective for children to release negative energy and start to focus.'

This strategy is similar to a progressive muscle relaxation meditation. As the muscles relax in the arms and hand, the tension leaves and it relieves stress. It also provides tactile stimulation that supports those children with sensory needs.

Teaching tip

Be aware that if you make your own stress ball, different fillers will feel different. A variety have been suggested so that children can choose the one they find most suitable.

Taking it further

Use the stress balls as part of daily guided meditations. This is especially effective for those children who find it hard to sit still for very long, as it gives them an active focus within the meditation.

Materials required:
- two party balloons
- filler (flour, salt, sugar, small beans/peas or rice)
- funnel
- scissors.

Assembly:
- Blow up the balloon so it inflates and stretches. Then let the air back out of the balloon.
- Using your funnel, fill the balloon with the chosen filler. Hold the end of the balloon tightly and stop when the filler reaches the neck of the balloon.
- Tie off the balloon with a knot.
- Cut the neck away from the second balloon and then stretch it over the first balloon, ensuring that the knot is completely covered. This second layer will help to prevent spillage should the first balloon get a tear.
- Decorate with permanent markers as desired.

How to use:
- Inhale and squeeze the ball tightly, focusing on how the ball feels in the hand and the burning felt in the tensed muscles.
- Exhale, mindfully noticing the feeling as the muscles relax.
- Repeat until feeling calm.

Encourage slow, deep breaths that allow the tension to be released throughout the body.

#MindfulStressBall

Mindful lap bag

'Perfect for my more active children who can't sit still for very long.'

Some children need extra support in being able to focus. A lap bag puts weight on a child's legs, allowing the child to feel more grounded. This pressure allows the child to mindfully focus on other things, like breathing, listening and observing.

Supplies needed:
- clean man's tube sock, preferably white if you are getting children to personalise.
- rice or dried beans – you will need a lot and it does depend on the size of the sock.
- needle and thread.
- permanent markers.

How to make a lap bag:
- Fill the sock with the rice or beans.
- Sew the top of the sock closed securely. You may want to double stitch. Then sew it one more time. You want to make sure that it is fidget-proof.
- Have the child decorate their own lap bag using the permanent markers.

How to use:
The lap bag should be laid across the top portion of the lap, near the hips. However, every child will be different, and some would rather have it in the centre of the lap or near the knees. Children should use it whenever they need to be more focused, particularly when doing schoolwork, listening to a lesson or doing a meditation. If it is being used to calm a child down, then, while they hold the lap bag, have them first focus on their deep breathing and then on the feel of the pressure of the bag.

Teaching tip

Add drops of relaxing essential oils like lavender. However, ensure that the child is not allergic to these.

Bonus idea ★

Use the lap bag as a heating pad. Microwave it for one minute. Check the temperature to ensure it is not too hot and then use it as normal, holding it in the hands or around the neck, which allows for greater relaxation and calmness.

#MindfulLapBag

Lovies

'The soothing nature of the lovies makes this my favourite mindfulness strategy for those children who are finding being mindful difficult.'

A lovie is a mindful sensory object that allows a child to self-soothe and bring focus to the present moment. This reduces the stress hormone cortisol, and reduces negative reactions.

Taking it further

Weighted lovie: Double the fabric, making a hem around the edges to attach the two squares, leaving a small section of a corner open. Turn it inside out and fill it with rice or beans. Secure the opening. The weight provides additional grounding to this sensory object.

Bonus idea ★

Giving children opportunities to make their own lovies allows for personalisation while also incorporating fine motor and sewing skills, depending on the age.

#Lovies

Stress makes the brain burn excess energy. When a child becomes overly stressed, their 'fight or flight' mode goes into overdrive. Objects can give children an active mindful focus in calming down and reacting in an appropriate manner.

Materials required:
- 30cm square piece of microfibre or fleece material – old blankets or scraps of material work well
- buttons, beads and different textured ribbons
- needle and thread.

How to make:
The edges of the square can be hemmed with a simple slip stitch. However, this is not required if using a fabric that does not unravel easily, like microfibre or fleece. Securely attach a few buttons, beads and pieces of ribbon around the square.

How to use:
Allow the children freedom to access their lovies, encouraging its use when you see their stress levels escalate. Have them hold, fold and rub it while getting them to breathe deeply and focusing only on how the lovie feels against their skin. Children who have a hard time focusing during meditation may find meditation easier with this object as a grounder.

Zen garden

'Mindful play at its best!'

Traditional Japanese Zen gardens are generally composed to represent the essence of nature and provide a gazing point for meditations. A Zen garden for children provides a small-world focus that allows them to explore natural materials through calm, relaxing play.

When the garden is completed, it adds the continued value of providing focus for meditation exercises.

Materials required:
- shallow tray
- dry sand
- polished rocks, seashells, small pieces of tree bark, small twigs
- craft sticks, for smoothing the sand.

How to use a Zen garden:
- Pour the dry sand into the shallow tray and place the natural items along the edge.
- Using the craft sticks, have the children smooth out the sand.
- The children should make tracks in the sand with their fingers and twigs.
- Have them arrange the items from nature in a pleasing pattern or design. They can trace paths around the shells and stones with their twigs. They should focus only on the present moment, and the lines being drawn and the elements being added.
- Once complete, have the children do a simple, one-minute breathing meditation as they focus on the sand, lines and objects.
- Repeat.

Teaching tip

Take pictures of the completed Zen gardens that children have created to use in Idea 85: Mindful corner or for a class meditation exercise similar to Idea 22: Mandala meditation.

Taking it further

Have children create larger Zen gardens in outdoor areas of provision, such as sand pits or beach play. The objects for design need to be equally large in size to balance the design, like larger stones, branches, leaves, etc. Use larger dowel rods, racks and shovels to create the lines.

#ZenGarden

Head massage

'This really does put the power of mindfulness in the child's own hands.'

Focused attention and massage on the head allows for greater focus and a reduction of stress.

Teaching children this simple head massage can provide a peaceful respite in an otherwise stressful situation while also developing a lifelong skill that will support their long-term well-being.

This head massage only requires use of a person's own hands.

- Play soft meditation music in the background and find a comfortable seated position.
- Before beginning, take three deep belly breaths, allowing the shoulders to relax on the exhale.
- Place the fingers of both hands across your forehead with your thumbs at the temples and middle fingers touching.
- Apply firm, gentle pressure with the fingers to the scalp while inhaling deeply and then exhaling as you release the pressure. Repeat three to four times.
- Move the fingers up into the hairline and again apply firm pressure and release three to four times.
- Continue to repeat the process as you move your fingers across your head. As you reach the back, your thumbs will not be able to remain on your temples; that is okay.
- Return fingers to the front of your head and to the sides. Repeat the press-and-release sequences as you move down the sides of your head.
- End by taking three deep belly breaths, allowing the shoulders to relax on the exhale.

#HeadMassage

Balancing butterflies

'A fun and creative mindful strategy!'

Calming techniques like 'balancing butterflies' allow children to focus and calm the restlessness they feel, and give them the ability to be in the present moment.

Materials required:
- A6 sheet of plain paper
- pencils, crayons and markers
- scissors
- tape
- thin cardboard (the thickness of a cereal box)
- two pennies.

How to make:
- Fold the A6 sheet of paper in half and draw half of a butterfly, including the head and tail, along the folded edge.
- While still folded, cut out the butterfly. Use it as a template to trace onto a piece of cardboard.
- Cut out the cardboard butterfly and decorate it with markers and crayons. Do NOT add anything that would add weight, like beads, sequins, buttons, etc.
- Turn the butterfly over and tape a penny onto the top of each wing, close to the head. Ensure that they are parallel to each other.

How to use:
- Turn the butterfly over so that the pennies are underneath and place your finger under the butterfly's head between the pennies. The butterfly should balance on your fingertip. Be patient to find the right finger placement.
- Take slow, deep breaths, focusing on the feel of the butterfly against the skin and the movement of body and breath to keep it balanced.

Teaching tip

Create a collection of flying insects and animals for children to use to mindfully balance. They must be symmetrical.

Taking it further

Have children balance the butterflies while taking a basic mindful walk (see Idea 88). Begin with mindful breaths and then focused mindful steps.

Bonus idea

Once the balancing on the finger is accomplished, try balancing it on other body parts like your nose!

#BalancingButterflies

Listening eggs

'A simple idea that is perfect for an area of provision that enhances both mindfulness and listening skills.'

This calming and relaxing activity requires children to be deliberate and careful in being present.

In order for children to communicate effectively, they must develop the core skill of listening. Mindful listening gives children this communication foundation.

Materials required:
- one empty egg carton for at least a dozen eggs
- coloured plastic eggs
- objects to place inside the eggs, such as small rocks, sand, paper clips, rubbers, beans, beads, etc.
- tape.

How to make:
- Place two similar objects inside two separate eggs and seal them shut with tape so the objects can't spill out.
- Number the eggs and objects in each egg and make a key to check the accuracy of the child's listening skills.

Activity:
- Place the eggs in the carton, ensuring that you mix them up.
- The child picks up each egg and gives it a little shake, listening to the sounds made.
- Once they have listened to the eggs, they can start matching the sounds by putting them in the carton side by side.
- Using the key, they can check the numbers to see whether they have matched the eggs correctly.
- The child mixes up the eggs and lets another child have a chance to match them.

#ListeningEggs

Superpowers, activate!

'Perfect for the youngest of children as it taps into their immense imagination.'

'Superpowers, activate!' is a simple strategy that children can use to remind themselves that they have the greatest superpower of all: the power to control their emotions and their reactions.

For the most part, children do live in the present. However, they also feel their emotions immediately and likewise tend to react immediately. They have little control over their lives, as adults tend to direct their entire days from the moment they get up in the morning, to when they go to bed.

Before explaining to children how to activate their mindful superpowers, take some time to discuss who their favourite superheroes are and what makes them so special. Then explain that you have a secret; they are all superheroes but they have not learned how to activate their powers, and today you will show them how tap into those special powers.

How to activate mindful superpowers:

- Each child should choose what their personal activation button is. It could be their temple, nose, ear, chin, scar, etc. It doesn't matter what it is. However, when they touch that button, their mindful superpowers will activate.
- When the children touch their activation button, they are to take three deep belly breaths and mindfully focus on their five senses: touch, taste, hearing, smell and sight. They should continue to quietly use their powers to focus as they continue to breathe deeply.

Teaching tip

When the class needs a mindful moment to calm down, announce loudly: 'Superpowers, activate!' Everyone stops and activates one of their superpowers for one minute. After a minute, announce loudly, 'Proceed!' and have the class get back to what they were doing but with a much calmer mind.

Taking it further

Design your own superhero: Each child can design their own mindful superhero. Make sure they include the superhero costume, colours and positive affirmations and then display the superheroes in the classroom.

#SuperpowersActivate

Mirror reflection

'I have noticed my class begin to actively use this strategy during break and lunch times. The concentration seen on their faces and the smiles that follow after successful completion make it worth the effort.'

Mirror reflection supports the development of mindful attention through slow, deliberate, mindful movements. These will also develop focus on attention as a leader and as a follower, which can support emotional development.

Teaching tip

Some children may get caught up in being *perfect* when doing this task and it takes away from the mindfulness of the activity. Remind them that this is not about being perfect but about paying attention. If it is not exactly right, that is okay.

Mindful attention is an important part of the development of mindfulness. The development of attention increases alertness, creates greater trust, develops tolerance and supports the identification of emotions in others. In addition, regular mindfulness practice develops better short-term memory, improved verbal reasoning and less mind-wandering.

- Divide the children into pairs, facing one another. Designate one child as the leader and one child as the follower.
- Begin the activity by doing a one-minute breathing meditation that calms the children and helps them to begin to focus their attention. Play soft meditation music in the background.
- Children should place their hands together, palm to palm. The leader then begins to make slow, deliberate movements with one hand and then another, with the other child following the movements and allowing their hands to move with the leader's. Movements can be up and down, side to side or in circles. Gently encourage attentive focus on the movement of the arms, the pressure of the hands and the warmth of the contact. Continue for as long as is appropriate for the children's age.

- Then, switch the roles of leader and follower and continue with the slow, deliberate movements.
- Again, switch roles and have children **close** their eyes so that they only have the touch of the hands as the cue to what to do. Encourage attentive focus on the movements.
- When both children have led the mirror reflections, have them sit tall and take three deep breaths.

After the activity, discuss it with the class:
- How did they feel in the beginning? Why?
- How did they feel doing the activity when their eyes were open? What about closed?
- What did it feel like to lead? What about to follow?
- How did they feel afterwards?

Encourage the discussion of emotions.

> ### Bonus idea ★
> Concentration sticks: This takes mirror reflection one step further in the development of mindful attention. Each pair needs two thin, straight sticks, equal in length (bamboo kebab skewers with their points cut off are perfect). Follow the same steps as in mirror reflections, but holding the sticks between each other using only one finger per hand. Keep the sticks firmly between the partners during the movements, focusing on the pressure of the fingers.

#MirrorReflections

Mindful smells

'A wonderful way to have children focus on the present moment mindfully.'

Through practice, mindful smelling can be a significant strategy, which can bring calm and relaxation to the children.

Taking it further

Different scents can have different effects on the mind and body. Some scents that boost a classroom's mindfulness include lavender, peppermint and rosemary for concentration, peppermint and orange for an energy boost, and orange, grapefruit and geranium for stress relief. Consider safe ways to introduce the scents into the classroom for added benefit.

The sense of smell has an important primary job of warning us about dangers, as well as allowing us to appreciate the beauty around us. The molecules that make up smells travel to the limbic system, which controls our heart rates, breathing, memory and blood pressure. It also controls our stress levels. Smells can be associated with our emotions, including good and bad memories.

Preparation:
Prepare four or five small containers for each group, each containing cotton balls that have been saturated with a scent, such as orange, mint, basil, lavender, vanilla or cinnamon (use the same scents for each group).

Activity:
- Divide the class into groups of no more than five children (the same as the number of scents).
- Set the ground rules for mindful smelling: no talking and no judging by making faces.
- Play some soft meditation music in the background and, on a given signal (bell), have each child open one of the scents.
- They should close their eyes and take three deep belly breaths, paying attention only to the smell. As they are smelling, ask them to silently consider what the scent reminds them of, what words describe it and what they think it comes from.
- Record their thoughts.
- Repeat until all the children have smelled all the scents.
- Afterwards, as a class, discuss their thoughts.

#MindfulSmells

Stone towers

'I have never seen so much concentration!'

Stone tower building is a mini-meditation. It gives children the opportunity to be quiet, think and focus just on what they are doing. Their silent, fixed attention is fully in the moment of balancing the stones.

When we think of mindfulness, many times our thoughts go directly to formal meditations. Guided meditations can be an integral part of developing mindfulness practice; however, you can also cultivate mindfulness informally by focusing attention on the moment to the sensations of individual activities. Doing one thing at a time and giving it your full attention allows you to slow down the process and be fully present in the moment as it unfolds, allowing recognition of all senses.

Materials required:
- a collection of stones of different sizes, ensuring that a large amount have some flatness on each side (also include a variety of colours and roundness)
- a few pictures of stone towers so that children get the idea of the task
- a quiet place to do the building
- optional: a camera so that the child can take a picture of their tower or paper and pencils so that they can make a sketch of their finished tower.

How to build a stone tower:
Challenge the children: 'How many stones can you use to make a tower?' There is no wrong or right way to build the stone tower. The key is to find the right stones that can be stacked or balanced on top of each other to create a tower of stones.

Teaching tip

Remind children to practise active, slow, deep breathing when they are stacking/balancing the stones. Then they should keep calm when the tower falls, close their eyes, take three mindful breaths and start again.

Taking it further

Get children to stack/ balance the stones by using a pair of chopsticks to pick up and put the stones in place. If the stones are simply too heavy, use small building blocks instead as part of the challenge.

#StoneTowers

Five finger relaxation

'After practising this strategy in the classroom, I started using it outside at break times in order to help children calm down during upsetting incidents between them.'

'Five finger relaxation' is a quick technique that combines deep breathing and positive affirmations to centre the child's thoughts and feelings.

How do we know children are stressed? The symptoms of stress in children can be seen in their irritability, moodiness, complaining, crying and withdrawal from activities. Once children have developed greater emotional intelligence, they will recognise these symptoms and take the necessary steps to calm themselves down. However, until that emotional intelligence is developed, adults can help by supporting the mindfulness practice.

When you notice the symptoms of stress:

- Turn one hand palm up with fingers spread.
- Inhale deeply and, on the exhale, fold the thumb into the palm and say 'I' to yourself.
- Inhale deeply and, on the exhale, fold the next finger into the palm and say 'am' to yourself.
- Continue with the next three fingers, individually saying, 'calm', 'and' and 'peaceful'.
- Repeat until you are feeling calm.

In order to embed this mindfulness strategy, use it as part of your transition procedure after break times or between lessons.

Taking it further

Discuss the symptoms of stress and how we can recognise when we are stressed. How does our head feel? How does our heart beat? What does our skin feel like? Does our breathing change?

Bonus idea ★

Positive affirmations are powerful tools in mindfulness development. Negativity can be deeply ingrained in one's mental make-up and positive affirmations can help to develop a positive mental attitude. Have children create their own five-word positive affirmation to use with this strategy. It may be something they want to get better at in class ('I am good at maths') or something that they want to improve behaviourally ('I can pay attention today').

#FiveFinger

A handful

'The children enjoyed using the five senses to focus them as they calmed down, and they became more specific in their descriptions the more times they took part in this strategy.'

'A handful' is a grounding technique that uses the five senses to manage overwhelming feelings or intense anxiety. It allows us to become aware of what is happening around us and be present in the moment, rather than allowing the feelings of chaos and distraction to take over. This shift in focus restores calmness.

When you notice the need to restore calm:

- Take a deep, cleansing belly breath.
- Make a tight fist, squeezing tightly and then relaxing the fist but not opening the hand.
- Open the hand one finger at a time, as if you were counting to five, and consider one of the five senses for each finger.
  - **Sight** – What do you see? What are the finer details? What colours do you see most?
  - **Hearing** – What do you hear? What is the smallest sound? What is a close sound? What is a sound that is far away?
  - **Smell** – What do you smell? How does the smell make you feel? What does the smell remind you of?
  - **Taste** – Can you taste anything even when you are not eating? What is the taste in your mouth? What is the texture of your taste buds?
  - **Touch** – What can you feel? What does it feel like? What is pleasant about how it feels? What is familiar about how it feels?
- Finally, take a deep, cleansing belly breath and smile.

Teaching tip

Practise this strategy before there is any major stress. Talking children through the senses helps them to develop the inner voice and questioning techniques that allow them to find that grounding focus. If you are supporting a child during a major stressful event, gently guide them through the strategy like a guided meditation, to provide structure to the moment.

#Handful

Not a drop!

'We did an art lesson using the "not a drop" game today! I have never had such a calm and successful art lesson that required lots of movement! Bliss!'

'Not a drop!' supports the development of self-awareness with a game-like quality.

Teaching tip

Playing soothing meditation music softly in the background can support the focus of the class in keeping calm throughout the activity.

Taking it further

Over time, have the children pretend that there is a bowl of water.

We live in a world of overstimulation. Technology is filled with chaotic images, loud sounds and constant movement. There is a growing lack of understanding of personal awareness and the effects we have on the people and environment around us.

The object of the activity is for children to be calm and considerate of their movements and actions, in order for them to complete their work in the area without spilling a drop of water!

- Place a bowl of water at least three-quarters full on each table.
- Explain that the children are going to play a game and the object of the game is to do their work without any water spilling or splashing out of the bowl.
- Discuss how this can be achieved. Examples include moving slowly, keeping to personal space, etc.
- Keep a tally of the number of spills that happen at each table.
- At the end of the given amount of time, determine the winning table.
- Children should discuss the strategies that they used to keep the water from spilling. How did they feel? What did the classroom feel like? How can we use these strategies when there isn't a bowl of water?
- Repeat the challenge at another time and see whether children can reduce the number of spills!

#NotADropGame

Mindful stories

'This is a great strategy to use with children who have pragmatic issues and need things very clearly spelled out for them.'

Mindful stories are effective in providing directions and guidance to children when dealing with a variety of social situations. Self-awareness, self-calming and self-management are encouraged by the specific social situations described in the stories.

Mindful stories can be used for an entire class or for individuals. However, there needs to be a clear mindfulness development moral to the story, with a personal focus that allows a child or children to learn how to deal with stressful situations mindfully.

- Decide on the focus and moral of the story.
- Choose a true situation that has occurred, such as an argument, angry outburst, temper tantrum, etc. Identify what was happening before and during the incident and use this as the basis of the story.
- Start the story by describing the incident, including where it occurs, who is involved, what they are doing and why they are doing this activity.
- Describe how the child or children are feeling during the incident and what their reactions are.
- In the next part of the story, remind children that they know many mindfulness strategies. They should choose one of the strategies to calm the incident down. Describe the strategy in detail.

Read the story:
- During story time, read the story.
- Discuss the moral of the story and when there might be other times that they can use this mindful strategy.

Taking it further

Over time, reread the story to the children as a reminder of the mindful strategies they can use in similar incidents.

Bonus idea

Make the mindful story into a book, adding illustrations or real photographs to use in your classroom's own mindful stories library.

#MindfulStories

Mindful corner

'The "mindful corner" is a well-used area of the classroom. I keep a watchful eye on who is using the area as it helps me identify those children who may be having a more difficult time in school or at home.'

A mindful corner is a space created with a variety of mindful activities that children can choose to use when they are feeling their emotions get out of control. It is a place where children can go to chill and relax.

Providing a space that children can retreat to in times of stress validates the importance of mindful strategies. Another important aspect of mindfulness development is a person's ability to identify what will support their ability to calm down.

Any activities added to this area need to be those that have been shared and practised in the class during previous sessions.

Must haves:
- a space away from the busiest activities
- comfortable seating and/or cushions
- mindfulness display reminding children of basic breathing techniques and positive affirmations
- ground rules for use of the area.

Possible activities:
- mindful colouring and doodling (see Part 7)
- stone towers (see Idea 80)
- lovies (see Idea 72)
- mindful story library (Idea 84)
- worry stones (see Idea 87)
- gratitude jar (see Idea 32)
- recorded meditations and headsets (Idea 10)
- finger labyrinth (see Idea 16)
- Zen garden (see Idea 73).

#MindfulCorner

Hand and wrist massage

'It focused the class on understanding that they have control over making themselves feel better and relaxed.'

Mindful hand and wrist massages allow children to relax their muscles, calm their breathing, improve their mood and reduce pain, stress, anxiety and tension by way of a natural reflex.

Before you begin:
- Set the mood by lowering the classroom lights and putting on some relaxing music.
- Explain to the children how this strategy can help them to calm down by focusing on the sensations.
- Encourage the use of deep breathing throughout to enhance the effects.

Teaching tip

Remind the children that all the motions need to be soft, with focus being on their breathing and the sensations they are feeling when they are massaging their hands.

How to:
- Sit up straight and take three deep, mindful breaths.
- Use the thumb to rub small, gentle circles around the opposite wrist, noticing the small bones and the sensations being felt.
- Use the thumb to continue to rub in small circles between the bones on the tops of the hands.
- Use the thumb in the same circular motion from the base at the palm to each fingertip.
- Pull each finger softly by the fingertip.
- Clasp hands together and move them back and forth and in circular motions.
- Turn the hand over and using the same circular motions, rub the palm, starting at the thumb base and working upwards.
- Repeat on the other hand.
- Complete the massage by giving your hand one more rub down like in the beginning.
- Lay your hands in your lap, take three deep breaths and continue your day.

#MindfulHandWrist Massage

Worry stones

'This is a great strategy for those children who are natural worriers.'

Worry stones are a focus object that allows a child to release their worry and connect with their inner mindfulness of calm and peace. These stones are polished and are small enough in size to easily hold in the hand and rub with your thumb, providing a self-soothing strategy.

Teaching tip

Polished river stones are well suited for this strategy and can be found in most discount stores.

Taking it further

Use the worry stones as a focus object for a simple breathing meditation. While playing soft meditation music, have the children begin by focusing on their breathing and then bringing their focus to the repetitive rubbing of the stone in their hand. Allow the meditation to continue for an age-appropriate amount of time.

#WorryStones

Rubbing the stone with the thumb is a form of reflexology, similar to Idea 86: Hand and wrist massage. Nerves in the thumb release natural endorphins, inducing relaxation and supporting the release of stress.

Worry stones are small enough to carry in your pocket, which allows for a quick mindfulness focus when needed.

Allow each child to select their own worry stone. They need to be comfortable with the stone. Encourage the children to try different ones by holding and rubbing them to find the one that feels best to them.

- When the child becomes distressed, anxious, upset or worried, they should take the worry stone in their hand and begin to rub the stone with their thumb.
- As they are rubbing, encourage them to take deep, mindful belly breaths, focusing only on the feel of the stone in their hands and the motion of their thumb as it rubs the smooth surface.
- If they have a specific worry, they can focus the worry into the stone and allow the stone to take it away or hold it for a little while.
- Once they are calm, they can put the stone away and continue.

Mindful walking

Part 9

Basic mindful walking

'I use this strategy when my class gets fidgety. It provides both exercise and focus for all the children.'

Mindful walking allows for a person to be present and purposeful in the present moment.

Sometime during the first 18 months of life, most of us pulled ourselves up on unsteady legs and took our first steps. During those tentative first steps, our minds were truly mindful of the position of our feet, the feel of the floor and the movement of our body. Concentration on walking – and only walking – happened with a clear, deliberate mind. Later, as we became more proficient at walking, the act became natural. There is now no thought as to what we are doing.

Basic mindful walking:
This should happen in a space large enough to accommodate your class. A hall or gym would be sufficient, but walking outside, particularly where there is nature around, can be the most rewarding.

- Children stand and take several belly breaths, allowing their bodies to relax from their heads to their toes.
- They should soften their eyes and fix their gaze on the ground about three metres ahead.
- Tell the children to smile slightly. Smiling signals to the brain that what is happening is pleasant.
- As they walk, have the children focus on the step of each foot as it rises up and then comes back down to the ground.
- Periodically, have the children stop and notice one object (flower, stone, stick, leaf,

etc.) or sound (bird chirping, water trickling, car passing, etc.) and spend a little time appreciating that one moment.

When children are used to basic mindful walking, try moving on to adding a beanbag.

Beanbag walking:
Clear, focused movements allow children to truly focus on the present moment. Beanbag walking encourages good posture while also requiring deliberate steps, with the focus being only on the weight of the beanbag on their head. For this activity, each child will need one beanbag. It is best to do this mindful walking inside and in bare feet.

- Children stand up straight, with heads up and looking straight ahead. Encourage them to imagine a string coming out of the top of their head, pulling their body up straight like a puppet.
- Children should take several belly breaths, allowing their bodies to relax from their heads to their toes.
- Then they should place one small beanbag on top of their head. Have them focus on the feel of the weight of the bag.
- They should soften their eyes and fix their gaze straight ahead, keeping the beanbag balanced on their head.
- As they walk, have the children focus on the step of each foot as it rises up and then comes back down to the ground, and the feel of the pressure of the beanbag on their heads.
- Continue to walk for the given amount of time.

Increase the challenge by asking the children to keep the beanbag on their heads while:
- doing a heel-toe walk
- walking around obstacles
- lowering the body to touch an object on the ground!

Taking it further

To give it added purpose, consider attaching mindful walking to a topic of study. Take a few minutes on a class trip to do a mindful walk, or consider your local community areas for a moment to practise their mindful walking skills.

#MindfulWalking

Rhythm of the bell

'I like using this strategy to calm my class and bring peace back to the room on bad weather days.'

Many people revert to pacing during times of distress and anxiety. Walking can be a soothing activity and bring peace of mind. For 'rhythm of the bell', you will need a bell or chime to use to provide the signal and pace of this mindful walking strategy.

Teaching tip

This strategy is a good mindful walking strategy to use when the weather is bad outside, as it can be used in smaller spaces such as a classroom.

Taking it further:

Add variety to this mindful walking strategy by chiming the bell in a slow, rhythmic pattern, with one step being taken per chime; adding a yoga pose to the sequence; adding a positive affirmation mantra to the sequence; or using this walking strategy as part of a walking labyrinth (see Idea 16).

#RhythmOfTheBell

- Children are to stand up straight but not stiff. Ask them to focus on how their feet feel as they touch the ground.
- They should curl their thumb in their left hand and wrap their other fingers around it as if they are holding their own hand. This will keep their arms from being a distraction by swinging as they walk.
- Get the children to soften their eyes and focus on the ground in front of them.
- Before beginning, have them take three deep belly breaths and, on the chime of the bell, they are to take three mindful steps, paying attention to how their feet touch the ground.
- They should then stop, take three deep belly breaths and wait for the bell to chime again.
- Repeat.
- Continue for an amount of time appropriate for your class.

Counting sounds

'Listening to the world around them opens up a whole new world that children didn't know was there!'

'Counting sounds' unites basic mindful walking with the act of active listening.

Children can find this purposeful focus extremely difficult. Our brains hum with a million different thoughts – multi-tasking is the norm, not the exception. The adrenaline from this leads to addiction to the stimulus and feeling lazy if we stop and focus on just one thing.

Mindful listening allows our brain to focus on the present moment, while mindful walking makes a basic connection between mind and body. Helping children to identify the connections allows us to support greater mindfulness development.

- Before beginning, have children stand up straight and take three mindful breaths. Guide them through the focus of inhaling deeply, holding the breath for a moment and then exhaling fully, allowing their shoulders to relax.
- Have children close their eyes and focus on just the sounds around them. How many different sounds can they hear?
- Guide them to focus on just one sound and think about it. Is it loud or soft? Is it made by a person, animal, machine, etc.? How does it make you feel?
- Children open their eyes and begin to walk, taking slow, deliberate steps, focusing on the feel of their feet as they touch the ground.
- Stop the children again and repeat the process as before, for as long as appropriate.
- End the session by having the children take three mindful breaths.

Taking it further

Allow the children time to discuss how many different sounds they heard and how those sounds made them feel.

#CountingSounds

Nature walking

'The fresh air and exercise is perfect for those children who require more active mindfulness strategies.'

Walking mindfully in nature brings us closer to nature and to our bodily movements. The slow, rhythmic movements help to relieve stress and calm the mind and body, while also providing the health benefits of exercise.

Teaching tip

Remind children that sometimes our attention drifts to other thoughts besides what we are supposed to focus on during the walk. This is okay. However, we should mindfully allow those thoughts to drift past us and refocus on the present moment.

Taking it further

Give each child a small bag to collect the objects noticed along the walk. Following the walk, the children can use the collected objects to sketch, paint or make into a collage, as part of a nature study. As part of an art display, the children can write about how they felt on their walk and how the objects made them feel.

- Have the children stand still, take three deep belly breaths and do a quick body scan (see Idea 8) in order to notice how their body feels as it stands, particularly how it feels for their body to be pressing down against the ground.
- Remind the children that their thoughts should remain on the walk and the beauty of nature around them.
- Get them to begin walking slowly, being aware of the heel-to-toe rhythm as their feet touch the ground.
- They are to focus their eyes softly forward as they walk.
- Stop them periodically and ask them to notice one NATURAL object, giving them time to notice the detail, colour, how it feels and how it smells.
- They should then take another mindful breath and continue walking.
- Repeat the walking and observing for a length of time that is appropriate for your class.
- Following the walk, have the children discuss what they saw on the walk and how it made them feel.

#NatureWalking

Follow the rainbow

'A simple but powerful strategy that really does bring colour into mindfulness development.'

Mindful walking is not about a destination; it is simply about each step and about breathing — being mindful in the moment! This strategy is useful when your class has become restless due to concentration levels, when they have been inside for a while or simply because the sun is shining!

'Follow the rainbow' is a fun twist to Idea 88: Basic mindful walking. It can be done individually, in pairs or in small groups, and keeps refocusing the children on the environment around them.

- Before beginning, review the basic colours of the rainbow. Use visual aids, such as pictures of rainbows or prisms, to allow children to create rainbows in the classroom. (This may be one session by itself.)
- Use Idea 88: Basic mindful walking as the basis to beginning the 'follow the rainbow' walk.
- After a short time, have the children stop and take a deep belly breath.
- Announce a colour for the children to notice. The children are to quietly look for the colour, focus on an object of that colour and take a deep belly breath.
- Have the children refocus and continue to walk.
- Again, stop the children after a short time, announce a different colour for children to notice and have them repeat the process.
- Continue until at least all the major colours have been identified.
- Afterwards, spend time discussing what objects children remember seeing for each colour and how the walk made them feel.

Teaching tip

Teach children a simple mnemonic to remember the order of the rainbow colours. Examples include 'Roy G Biv' and 'Richard of York Gave Battle in Vain'.

Taking it further

Give each child a sketch sheet or journal page to draw/write the objects that they notice during their 'follow the rainbow' walk. Use this to create a display or book to use in the classroom or Idea 85: Mindful corner.

#FollowTheRainbow

Teacher's mindfulness

Part 10

One-minute breathing meditation

'This is my number one mindfulness strategy. When I start to feel as if everything is happening at once and making me feel out of control, this is what I try first!'

Breathing is one of the most natural things a person can do, and an automatic reflex that is hard-wired in our brains. The one-minute breathing meditation is simple and takes little time but has big benefits!

Mindful breathing changes energy from tension to relaxation by turning off our sympathetic nervous system, which produces stress hormones. This turns on our parasympathetic nervous system, turning off the stress hormone pump. Thus, deep breathing relaxes the body, decreases heart rate, lowers blood pressure and creates a feeling of calmness.

- Sit or stand comfortably.
- Close your eyes.
- Bring your attention to your breath.
- Breathe in deeply, filling your abdomen as you inhale. Hold the breath for a moment and then exhale fully.
- Focus your attention on your nostrils and notice the inhale and exhale of air, how it feels and how it makes your body feel.
- Continue for 15 breaths. This will be approximately one minute.

Other thoughts will begin to fill your mind as you are breathing, especially when you first begin using this strategy. That is okay! Acknowledge the thought, praise yourself for noticing it and allow it to float away without judgement or more attention. Over time, you will find there are fewer thoughts passing through your head during the meditation.

#OneMinuteMeditation

100 breaths

'This simple meditation allows me to relax through focused breathing while also developing the mindful practice of being in the present moment.'

Research has shown that ten minutes of mindful practice every day for eight weeks can grow specific areas of the brain by 25%. The natural relaxation technique '100 breaths' provides a mindful anchor on a day-to-day basis, with calming attributes that can easily take you to your ten minutes of mindfulness in a day.

- Sit or lie comfortably in a place where you can be undisturbed for ten to 15 minutes.
- Close your eyes and allow your shoulders to relax.
- Take ten deep, mindful breaths, focusing only on the breath: the feeling of the air as it is inhaled through the nose and the warmth of the air as it is exhaled.
- Allow your mind to wander to other thoughts for two seconds, and then let them drift away as you refocus on your breathing.
- Take ten more deep, mindful breaths and then let your mind wander again.
- Repeat the process until you have taken a total of 100 breaths.

Taking it further

Instead of counting the breaths, set a timer for ten minutes, play soft meditation music and then focus on the breaths you take. Allow yourself to feel each breath as you inhale and exhale. Once the timer goes off, your meditation is complete. If any random thoughts float through your mind during the meditation, acknowledge the thought and allow it to pass through your mind without judgement.

#100Breaths

Mindfulness to-do list

'I am terrible at remembering to practise mindfulness, even when I know it is good for me. The 'mindfulness to-do list' helps keep me on track during the day.'

We all need to give ourselves some time and care to look after ourselves. The mindfulness to-do list does this.

Spending time to mindfully enjoy your life and family gives your working mind time to recuperate after a busy week. It allows us to be more considerate of our actions rather than those actions becoming unmindful reactions.

It doesn't take a lot of time to be mindful; it just takes practice and, sometimes, a few reminders.

- Take one minute, close your eyes and breathe deeply. Do this several times a day. Try Idea 93: One-minute breathing meditation.
- Observe your thoughts and feelings without judgement. Our thoughts are not always kind to us. Take a moment to notice the thought but don't judge it. Acknowledge the thought and proceed.
- Focus on the present moment and note one specific detail. Our minds are swirling with thoughts as they jump between conversations that happened yesterday to things we need to do tomorrow. Stop for a moment and just notice what is happening right now, in this moment.
- Think of five things that you are thankful for in your life. Exploring and celebrating gratitude allows us to mindfully consider the good things in life in a variety of ways. Supporting and encouraging the development of the 'bright side of life' gives us the ability to evaluate life with more balance.

#MindfulnessToDoList

Mindful hand-washing

'This is my quick-fix, go-to strategy when just deep breathing doesn't work. Giving myself a few minutes of self-indulgence allows me to take back control of my emotions and continue with the day.'

Mindful hand-washing is a painless shock therapy that uses the warmth of the water to relax the mind and body.

Many psychologists believe that our emotions begin with a physical sensation, positive or negative. When we focus on positive sensations that are calming, we can become calm emotionally. Sometimes, despite our best efforts to be mindful and keep our emotions in check, we just can't seem to hold back the racing heart, the swirling negative thoughts and the feelings of fight or flight.

When you wash your hands in warm water, it opens the blood vessels and tricks your brain out of a stressful state.

- When you go to wash your hands, be mindful of the sensation of the water and soap as your rub your palms, between your fingers and on top of your hands. Breathe deeply, allowing your breathing to enhance the feel of the water and soap.
  - How does this moment feel?
  - How is it making the rest of your body feel?

Taking it further

Fill the bowl or the sink with warm water. Once full, immerse your hands in the water, taking deep, mindful breaths and focusing on the feel of the water on your hands and fingers. Softly swirl your hands in the water, allowing the water to move over your hands and between your fingers.

Bonus idea

If you don't have access to warm water, rub your hands together quickly to warm them up. The heat produced from the friction will have a similar effect to the warm water.

#MindfulHandWashing

Meditation group

'This is probably the most valuable skill I've learnt in four years of teaching. Why? It's had a massive impact on my performance in the classroom and, most importantly, at home as a dad and a husband.'

Ten-minute daily meditations in the morning can help you start the day in a calm, mindful mood, supporting the day's work. However, you will find that meditating on your own can be as difficult as exercising on your own, while meditating in small groups provides focus and support on the road to mindfulness development.

Taking it further

Try out a number of different kinds of meditations over the first few weeks. Try body scans, loving kindness, breathing, gratitude, peace, anxiety, etc. Identify the favourites for the group. Take turns to choose a meditation for the day.

Mindfulness is a purposeful act, and the process of becoming mindful can seem selfish in today's society, which deems multi-tasking as what people do to become successful. This is particularly true for educators as we juggle children, parents, other teachers and leaders, and government expectations.

With a growing focus on staff well-being, identifying good, cost-effective ways of supporting the mental health of ourselves and colleagues has become a priority on many agendas, and a meditation group provides like-minded support.

- Identify a number of ten-minute guided meditations that are readily accessible. There are many free meditations online as well as useful examples within meditation and mindfulness apps.
- Identify a comfortable place and time for daily meditation sessions. Mornings before school are good. Most people who meditate before the day starts find the meditations very beneficial.
- Advertise! Encourage! Share!
- Be faithful to the meditation – make sure that you go!

#MeditationGroup

Mindful reflection

'Mindful reflection has reminded me of the importance of appreciating even the smallest things and smallest successes.'

Mindful reflection requires you to think deeply or carefully about something on a daily basis. When we take part in mindful reflection, we are taking the opportunity to be present in the moment of the day and developing a habit of assessing our personal and work lives.

With the hustle and bustle of a busy day in the classroom, there seems to be little time to reflect. Add to this the pull of social media, phones, emails, etc., and our day is consumed by the completion of tasks with no time to add some introspection. This self-reflection is an important skill to develop as part of our everyday lives.

- Buy yourself a nice notebook. Choose one that is a symbol of your personality and brings a smile to your face when you see the pattern and colours.
- Each day, take a few minutes to reflect on the day and write down four things. The reflections can be a few words, a drawn picture, a souvenir or a narrative. They can be as short or as long as you want them to be.
- Ensure that three of the reflections are positive and only one is negative. The positivity ratio supports our emotional intelligence development. It allows us to find a balance in our lives by acknowledging the negatives but not allowing them to take over.

Taking it further

On days when you are finding it the most difficult, take a few extra minutes to look back on your reflections. Allow yourself to be immersed in the good memories you have collected over time and accept the negatives that have occurred. Remind yourself that there is a lot to be thankful for in your life and enjoy just being.

#MindfulReflection

Everyday mindfulness

'My mind is no longer full. I am calm, happy and ready to face the challenges of the day – thankful, positive and smiling.'

Many times when I speak to people about practising mindfulness, they say they 'just don't have time'. Actually, people who practise mindfulness express that the more mindful they are during the day, the more time they actually gain during that day.

The reduction of stress, energy and time spent on past/future thoughts, and increased periods of calmness allow for more effective time-management. During the day, there are periods of time when you multi-task or go into autopilot, filled with mindless thoughts. Instead of allowing mindless thoughts to take over, use this time to become more mindful.

Mindful object:
Once you are dressed for the day, choose an item you are wearing to be your mindful object. It can be a ring, your ID badge, a necklace, tie, shoes, your watch, a button on your shirt, etc. It doesn't matter what it is, as long as it is something you will see several times.

During the day, at any point you notice your mindful object, touch it and take three deep, mindful breaths, paying attention to the air flowing in and out your body.

Brushing teeth:
This is about being in the present moment, from the preparation of your toothbrush to rinsing your mouth. Here are some prompts to be mindful of while you are going about this everyday task.

- How does your toothbrush feel in your hand? Is the grip smooth or rough?
- How does the balance change when you put the toothpaste on the brush?
- What does the toothpaste smell like?

- How do the bristles feel against your teeth? Your tongue? Your cheek and gums?
- Notice the foaming of the toothpaste in your mouth and how it feels.
- How does your tongue feel against your freshly brushed teeth? Can you still smell or taste the toothpaste? How do you feel now?

Time for a drink:
Millions of cups of coffee and tea are made around the world every day. Most of the time, they are quickly made and drunk with little or no awareness. This is one of those everyday activities that you can use to develop your mindfulness.

- Make your coffee or tea as normal.
- Sit down with your beverage and allow yourself to be aware of at least the *first few minutes of drinking*.
- Take a deep breath of the steam coming from your drink. Take in the aroma.
- Look at your drink. What colour is it? How does the surface of the drink look?
- Take a sip. Allow the sip to linger in the mouth. Notice the warmth of the liquid against your tongue, cheeks, gums and palate. What can you taste?
- Continue to be mindful of each sip, allowing yourself to be in the very present moment of drinking.

Smile:
Every day, your brain keeps track of your smiles. It knows how often you've smiled and which overall emotional state you are in.

On average, children smile over 400 times a day. Whilst happy adults still smile 40 to 50 times a day, the average, however, is only about 20 times.

- Be mindful of your smiles today. Were they self-motivated or due to a reaction from seeing others smile?
- Notice how your body feels when you smile. Does your mental state change, even just for a moment?
- Does smiling get easier as the day goes on?

Taking it further

Consider other activities you participate in on a daily basis – taking a shower, walking to work, washing the dishes, etc. How can you make those times of mindfulness?

#EverydayMindfulness

121

Mindful daydreaming

'I have found that my daydreams have become one of my favourite meditation sessions. I have walked along beautiful beaches, watched amazing sunsets and floated in calm seas.'

Mindful daydreaming makes the daydreams the object of the mindful focus.

Taking it further

Keep a mindful daydream journal, noting the daydreams and how these daydreams made you feel. Over time, be mindful of any patterns to your daydreams, particularly those that support your improved emotional well-being.

When we are mindful of our daydreams, we are able to:

- Receive feedback on our own conscious or unconscious well-being. Our spontaneous daydreams can help us to know whether we are more positive or negative in the moment, depending on the emotions evoked by the daydream.
- Manipulate our thoughts allowing us to engage with our emotions without physical risk.
- Take a mini-holiday allowing us to explore places that bring us peace and relaxation. This may be a particular landscape, activity or alternative reality.

If we mindfully daydream, we are bringing focus, formality and purpose. Treat these daydreams as a meditation.

- Find a quiet place and sit or lie in a comfortable position where you will not be disturbed.
- You may want to set a timer to give a definite time to this meditation or you can use this as a bedtime meditation to fall into a peaceful sleep.
- Play soft meditation music and take deep, mindful breaths.
- Allow your mind to roam without any specific purpose.
- As the thoughts come through, pay attention to them but do not judge. Just note them and allow them to flow.

#MindfulDaydreaming